LARGE OVAL TRAY. DETAILS FOR DECORATING
ARE SHOWN IN PLATES 31 THROUGH 34.

PENNSYLVANIA DOWER CHEST WITH TWO BRIDE BOXES
(Courtesy of Metropolitan Museum of Art)

American
Antique Decoration

by

ELLEN S. SABINE

WITH DRAWINGS BY THE AUTHOR
PHOTOGRAPHS BY HILDA BORCHERDING

BONANZA BOOKS
NEW YORK

517114577
Copyright © MCMLVI by D. Van Nostrand Company, Inc.
Library of Congress Catalog Card Number: 56-12094
All rights reserved
This edition is published by Bonanza Books
a division of Crown Publishers, Inc.
by arrangement with the author
a b c d e f g h
Manufactured in the United States Of America

Foreword

For the amateur artist, the hobbyist, or the lover of antiques this book will prove to be a valuable guide to the old-new art, known as American Antique Decoration. The author, Ellen Sabine, defines the techniques, enumerates the materials, and describes the procedures in such simple, easy-to-understand words that the reader will be enticed to begin, and encouraged to perfect, the skills which re-create this early American art.

While Mrs. Sabine clearly explains each step in the process of creating a beautiful object, she anticipates the problems and pitfalls and sets forth all the requisites for successful achievement. Her informal directions are detailed, enabling the student to progress with confidence from the simplest to the most elaborate work.

For several years Mrs. Sabine has shared her artistic knowledge and skill with many hundreds of students in her classes at Central Branch YWCA in New York City. Her explicit directions and her love for this art form have brought the joy of new creative experiences to these students. She tells her students that practice is essential in learning a new skill, and she reminds them that "All the practice in the world is of no use if you keep thinking that you'll never be able to do it."

Now this knowledge and skill are placed at your disposal in this book. You will be inspired and encouraged to try your hand and brush. As you work, you may find it helpful to heed this bit of philosophy which Mrs. Sabine is in the habit of saying to her students. "Keep in your mind's eye a picture of yourself as doing beautifully whatever it is you want to do. This mental attitude of success, coupled with practice, is the only recipe (I know of) that can make an artist of you or anyone, and if followed implicitly it will assure success!"

CLARICE L. HAINES
Director of Adult Education
Central Branch, Y.W.C.A.
New York, N. Y.

Preface

It has always been a marked characteristic of human beings that they have sought to decorate their immediate surroundings. In certain parts of the world there are caves the walls of which were decorated by men of prehistoric times, and some of the surviving work shows a high standard of artistic skill. Weapons and utensils were similarly painted and carved.

With the coming of houses and other advances of civilization the scope for decoration was correspondingly enlarged. Even when machines of iron and steel arrived on the scene, they were frequently decorated in an elaborate manner, of which many an old sewing machine is an example.

Although the forms of decoration may change as time goes on, the urge to decorate never entirely disappears. Modern living, which is increasingly altering our ways in so many respects, calls no less than earlier times for the compensation of decoration. Dreary indeed would be a purely utilitarian world from which every "unnecessary" adornment was banished! If, then, one is asked, "Why decorate?" the answer must surely be, "Because we like it." Immense as are the changes which the industrial age has brought about, it has left the realm of artistic expression little affected. There the machine is no substitute for the human hand and eye, and the urge to artistic creation cannot be satisfied by the most ingenious touch-of-a-button invention. That is why people constantly seek out creative handicrafts. They refuse to let their personalities be submerged by the merely mechanical and automatic.

If a thing of beauty is a joy forever, it is doubly so to the person who created it. To be an artist in American Antique Decoration, one need not be an artist in the full sense, a professional who devotes all his faculties to art and undergoes years of training. A keen desire to learn and to do will carry the amateur far in this field.

There exists for our use a vast storehouse of fascinating designs, taken from old pieces of furniture and other household objects. These designs are as much a part of our national heritage as the Declaration of Independence. To use them is not an "escape into the past," for they are already a part of us and of our traditions. Most of them are truly beautiful, and a conscious appreciation of their worth and importance is an inspiring and enriching experience for anyone.

It is true that we decorate because we like it. But a beautifully decorated home gives something more than immediate pleasure to the eye. It has far-reaching effects on the people who live there, encouraging thoughts and feelings of well-being and contentment. Since the subconscious mind is always influenced by its surroundings, it is wisdom to make those surroundings beautiful. This book offers guidance to those who wish to use American Antique Decoration in beautifying their homes, and it will also be found helpful by the collector and restorer of antiques.

ACKNOWLEDGMENTS

My grateful thanks are tendered to Mrs. Eda Baum, Mrs. Wesley S. Block, Jr., Mrs. Grosvenor Farwell, Miss Katherine Hatch, Mrs. Edward Herndon, the Index of American Design (National Gallery of Art, Washington, D.C.), Mrs. George E. Jones, Mrs. Alan Kissock, Mrs. John G. McTernan, the Metropolitan Museum of Art (New York), Mrs. Victor Mravlag, the New York Public Library, the Queens Borough Public Library (Jamaica, N.Y.), Mrs. W. Mason Smith, Jr., Miss Nadine Stein, Mrs. Louis Stevenson, Mrs. Arthur S. Tompkins, and Mrs. Marion Wood for their kind permission to use designs and for supplying information; to Mrs. Roderick D. MacAlpine for special help on many occasions; to my sister, Miss Hilda Borcherding, for the photographs; to Mr. Richard Gray for aiding in their production; and to my husband for assisting in the preparation of the manuscript. Finally, I would like to record the immense debt which all who are engaged in this field owe and will always owe to the late Esther Stevens Brazer, and to the Esther Stevens Brazer Guild of the Historical Society of Early American Decoration, which was founded in her memory.

E. S. S.

Contents

List of Illustrations

PHOTOGRAPHS

(Photos. I to XI between pp. 22-23; Photos. XII-XIX between pp. 38-39)

American
Antique Decoration

COUNTRY TINWARE

1 Techniques and Their History

Five main techniques are employed in American Antique Decoration, namely, Country Painting, Freehand Bronze, Stenciling, Floating Color, and Gold Leaf. Each of these will be dealt with later in a separate chapter, and here we shall give them a brief preliminary survey. With the exception of stenciling, all of them are rated as freehand techniques. But although the freehand techniques are carried out without the aid of a stencil, the designs are first traced on the surface to be decorated, and so you have an outline to follow when you begin to paint.

Country Painting was used in the old days to decorate the many household articles made by the tinsmith. From about 1740 English tinplate was imported and was made here into trays, various boxes, candle holders, coffee pots, tea pots, canisters, tea caddies, and many other things. Such items formed part of the stock of country peddlers, who were welcome visitors to every farm and village, for they brought not only their tinware and other goods, but, no less important, the news and gossip from other places.

It was not long before it was discovered that decorated pieces sold more readily than undecorated ones. The painted surfaces were not only more attractive, but they prevented rusting. This early painting technique was used also, though to a less extent, for the decoration of chairs, chests, wooden boxes, and other household articles.

Country painting is good for the soul. It is gay and colorful; its very simplicity of arrangement and its flat, posterlike colors seem to be a healthy antidote for the complexities of modern living. It is always delightful to do and delightful to live with. It seems to fit in almost anywhere.

Freehand Bronze painting is a method of applying bronze powders over an underpainting that is partly dry. Sometimes the entire pattern is covered with the powder, and sometimes only highlights, thus leaving portions of the underpainting to show and to form part of the design. Details of line and color are added later.

Freehand bronze is a more sophisticated type of decoration than country painting. It is often found in conjunction with gold leaf, and sometimes with stenciling. Occasionally two or three different shades of bronze powders were used.

It is a very old technique and undoubtedly originated in the East. Many eighteenth-century European and American pieces show Oriental influence in their delicacy of design and treatment. Freehand bronze was used a

1

great deal on trays and furniture. Since, however, it required considerable skill and ample time, new and more rapid methods of decoration became more popular, and early in the nineteenth century it more or less ceased to be employed.

Stenciling is one of the most satisfying and fascinating of the old techniques. Its main development was during the period from about 1815 to 1850, and it was used on Boston rockers, Hitchcock and other chairs, pianos, wardrobes, trays, mirrors, cornices, chests, beds, boxes, and many other domestic pieces. The earlier examples are often elegant and formal. The designs include beautifully cut motifs and delicate shading and evince great artistry of arrangement. As the years went on, however, economic necessity drove the stencilers to devote less time to their work and to employ simpler designs and methods. This trend continued until the work done around 1850 was often quite crude.

Stenciling can be used with great effect in our homes today. One can decorate as simply or as intricately as one pleases, and once a stencil is cut, the speed with which it can be used in decorating an object is remarkable. There are few styles of room in which stenciling does not seem appropriate. A simple leaf repeated to form a border around the edge of a modern table, for example, never fails to add interest and charm.

Floating Color is a method used to produce a subtle blending of colors which can be achieved in no other way. Generally it is used in the painting of flowers or fruits that require a soft blending of transparent colors over an underlying pattern of opaque color. These colors are actually floated on a mixture of varnish and linseed oil. The result of these glazes is to produce a depth and a glow that are most pleasing.

Examples of floating color are found on old lace-edge and Chippendale trays and on some rectangular ones. This technique was also used on furniture and other household articles. As it required considerable skill, it is generally found to have been used on the finer pieces, often in conjunction with gold leaf. No one should attempt to do floating color who has not had considerable practice in country painting.

Gold Leaf. The sheer beauty and elegance of gold leaf put it in a class apart. Early eighteenth-century England used it to imitate the expensive lacquer ware imported from the East. From this period have come down very elaborate gold leaf trays which were imported by the American colonists. Naturally, it was not long before American artists too began to decorate with gold leaf, and they used it until well into the nineteenth century. In the domain of furniture, chairs in particular were decorated with gold leaf, sometimes for the whole design, as on Sheraton fancy chairs, and sometimes only for parts of the design, as on the finer type of Hitchcock chairs. It was used also with notable effect on rockers, tables, highboys, etc.

2

The application of gold leaf requires a certain skill in applying the underpainting, and also in the handling of the gold leaf itself. However, as in other fields, patience and a degree of practice will be well rewarded and will result in good technique. An effect of splendor combined with good taste is given to the home which contains objects adorned with gold leaf.

2 Materials and Their Care

The following are the essential materials required for American antique decoration work, together with some comments on their care.

Tube Colors: (a) Japan Colors in tubes of Vermilion (light), Chrome Green (light), Chrome Yellow (medium), and Lamp Black.

(b) Artists' Oil Colors in small tubes of Alizarin Crimson, Prussian Blue, Burnt Sienna, Burnt Umber, Raw Umber, Yellow Ochre, and Indian Yellow or Yellow Lake. Also a medium-sized tube of Titanium White or Superba White. Note that the Alizarin Crimson, Prussian Blue, Indian Yellow, and Yellow Lake differ from the others in that they are transparent colors.

The Japan colors were originally ground in Japan and were used in the West by the old coach painters. They are opaque and dry and give a flat, smooth surface. The tubes should be handled carefully, as they crack easily, with the result that the paint soon dries and becomes useless.

Keep the caps on all tubes when not in immediate use. If a cap sticks, do not try to unscrew it by a degree of force that will twist the tube. Instead, hold the cap for a few seconds only in the flame of a match. The warmth will cause it to expand, and using a cloth to protect your fingers, you can invariably unscrew it.

Bronze Powders: Palegold Lining, Deepgold, Aluminum (silver), and Fire.

Gold Leaf: 1 book of mounted pale gold.

Tracing Paper: 1 roll, thin and very transparent, 21 inches wide.

Frosted Acetate: 1 roll, medium weight. This is a transparent plastic sheet, one side of which is slightly frosted so that it will take paint. Its transparency enables one directly to copy a pattern underneath it without having first to trace an outline.

Black Drawing Ink.

Crow-quill: A fine-pointed pen.

Drawing Pencils: H, 2H, and 4H.

Architect's Tracing Linen: 1 yard. Although the old stencilers used paper, stencils for the projects in this book will be made from architect's linen, the kind that has a shiny undersurface. This sturdy fabric will last almost indefinitely, provided it is properly cared for. It should be kept away from all forms of moisture, which dissolves the starch lining and renders the linen useless for stenciling purposes. Cut stencils should be kept in wax paper envelopes, which can be made from wax paper sheets,

4

folded and secured with cellophane tape. They should be kept lying flat. Immediately after using stencils, clean them on both sides with Carbona cleaning fluid and a soft cloth. They dry in a few minutes.

Stencil Scissors: These are cuticle scissors, but with *straight* blades. They may be obtained from various sources, one of which is Meilinger and Sons, 913 Eighth Avenue, New York 19, N.Y., for a few dollars, the price of which includes the special sharpening necessary for stencil cutting. Very small embroidery scissors may be used if they are specially sharpened.

Don't try to cut stencils with an inadequate pair of scissors; it takes all the joy out of an otherwise delightful pastime.

Mohair: You will need a piece about 9 by 12 inches of this high-piled upholstery fabric to use as a "palette" for holding the bronze powders. Overcast or blanket-stitch the edges to prevent fraying. The bronze powders are placed along the lengthwise center fold, as shown in Plate 4. When not in use, the palette should be folded in half lengthwise, rolled up tightly crosswise, and secured with a small elastic band. The high pile and the tight rolling will keep the different-colored powders from mixing.

Velvet: 3-inch wide satin-backed black velvet ribbon is used to apply the bronze powders. Three or four pieces, each 4 inches long, should be prepared. On each piece, sew the two rough edges together to form a cylinder with both selvage ends open. These are known as "velvet fingers." Keep one for freehand bronze, one for gold stenciling, and one for aluminum powder.

Black Paper: For stenciling this may be prepared by tacking ordinary shelf paper in convenient lengths to sheets of newspaper, using small pieces of masking tape at the corners. Give the shelf paper two thin coats of flat black paint, allowing at least 24 hours for each coat to dry. For directions on thinning the black paint, see Chapter 3. Black paper is used for copying stencil patterns and for practice work.

There is a commercial black paper suitable for our purpose, which is called "Hazenkote Black" (sold by the Hazen Paper Company of Holyoke, Mass.). However, it comes only in a large roll, which is more than an individual needs. Teachers, institutions, and groups find such a roll economical.

Varnish: Varnish is used as a medium for mixing tube colors in the painting of designs, for finishing coats on a decorated piece, and for stenciling. Pratt & Lambert #61 Floor Varnish, clear gloss, is a good-quality varnish which I use with good results. Whenever varnish is mentioned in this book, this is the quality of varnish intended, unless otherwise indicated. A number of other fine varnishes are on the market which expert decorators have found to work beautifully, among them McCloskey's, Murphy's, Pierce's. It should be noted, however, that not every varnish is suitable for stenciling, particularly some of the heavier kinds.

5

Varnish should never be stirred. The ½ pint size is handiest. So long as the can has not been opened, the contents will keep in a perfect state. On contact with the air, the spirits begin to evaporate, and once the varnish has definitely begun to thicken, it should not be used. Since it cannot be retrieved, proper care should be taken from the first to ensure that no needless waste occurs. It is obvious that the cover should be kept on the can when it is not in use. But be sure that the cover is on *tightly*—step on it to make quite sure. When a can is one-third used, it is a good plan to pour the rest of the varnish into small bottles with good screw caps, since the air in the can, even though it is tightly closed, will thicken the varnish.

Primer: A high-grade metal primer paint which dries quite smooth and thus requires very little sandpapering should be used. It should be stirred thoroughly before using and may be thinned with turpentine. Pratt & Lambert's Effecto Enamel Primer is among the better-grade primer paints.

When you have finished applying a coat of paint, wipe off the rim of the can with a cloth. Then pour a little turpentine on top of the paint in the can, just enough to cover the surface, letting it float there. This will prevent a skin forming. Then replace the lid and press it down tightly. The next time you open the can, simply mix the turpentine in with the paint, and it will probably thin it just enough for use.

Flat Black Paint: Pratt & Lambert's Sta-Blac *Flat* Enamel is an excellent well-covering flat black. It should be cared for in the same way as the primer. Sherwin-Williams, Lowe, and Sapolin are among other makers of high-quality flat black paints.

Brushes: (a) For applying coats of varnish and background paints, ordinary one-inch flat bristle brushes as sold in paint stores at a nominal price can be used. Some decorators, however, prefer to use better-quality brushes for this work and find them worth the extra cost. In any event, it is of the first importance to keep the brush in perfect condition.

To clean a varnish brush, first wipe it off thoroughly with newspaper. Then douse it up and down in a dry cleaning fluid such as Energine, letting it stand in the fluid about 15 minutes, with enough fluid to cover the hairs. After this, wash the brush thoroughly in soap and water, and rinse it well. Shake out the surplus water, and shape the brush carefully. Stand it up in a jar to dry undisturbed. The dry cleaning fluid can be kept in a screw-top jar, and used again and again.

To clean a paint brush, wipe it off thoroughly with newspaper, and then clean it in turpentine, letting it stand in the spirit 10 or 15 minutes. Wash the brush thoroughly with soap and water, and rinse. Shake out the surplus water, and shape the brush. If you intend to use the brush again the next day, it need not be cleaned, but may be left standing overnight in turpentine, or in plain water, with just enough of the fluid to cover the hairs.

(b) For painting designs, we require: (1) *Square-tipped ox-hair rigger or showcard brushes* #4 or #5. Hairs should be ⅝ to ¾ inch long. Buy two for convenience. (2) *Square-tipped camel's-hair quill brushes,* #0 and #1. Hairs should be ¾ inch long. (3) *Striper.* This is a square-tipped quill brush with hairs about 1½ inches long, and about the thickness of a #1 quill. It is used without a handle.

To clean these brushes, wipe them gently with a cloth, and then douse them up and down in Carbona Cleaning Fluid. Let them stand in the fluid about 15 minutes, so that any paint that has worked up into the ferrule is soaked out. Then wash thoroughly in soap and water, and rinse. Shake out surplus water, shape carefully, and stand up in a jar undisturbed until they are dry.

Turpentine: 1 quart.

Steel Wool: #000.

Sandpaper: #000 or very fine.

Crude Oil: Pint bottle from paint store.

Decorator's Masking Tape: 1 roll.

Carbona Cleaning Fluid: 1 bottle. Examine label carefully for this exact wording, that is, Carbona Cleaning Fluid, as the Carbona company makes other cleaners useless for our purpose.

Energine: 1 bottle. This is a dry cleaning fluid sold in most stores.

Linseed Oil: 1 small bottle from an artist supply store.

Powdered Pumice: 2-oz size from a drugstore.

Magnesium Carbonate: 1-oz cake usually available at a drugstore.

Deoxidine: #624. This is a rust remover sold by Bricker & Andes, 290 Atlantic Avenue, Brooklyn 2, N.Y., at $1.50 for a quart, and $4 for a gallon. Comparable rust removers may be also available from other suppliers.

Bottle Caps: Start saving bottle caps about 1 inch in diameter and ½ inch high—for example, those that come on catsup bottles. Bottle caps make convenient-sized receptacles for the varnish used in painting designs.

Empty Jars and Bottles: Collect some small jars or bottles, about 2 or 3 inches deep, which have good, airtight screw tops. These will be needed for holding varnish, Carbona Cleaning Fluid, "slow varnish," etc. Bronze powders which come in packets are handled more conveniently if they are transferred to small bottles or jars. Cold-cream jars and others of similar type are useful for holding the mixed background colors.

Newspapers: Always have plenty of newspapers on hand. You will need them to spread over your work tables, to wipe brushes, and to use as "palettes" in painting designs.

Many artist supply stores carry items that the American antique decorator can use. The following list of some of the suppliers is included for your convenience. Several of them carry trays.

Joseph Mayer Co., 5-9 Union Square West, New York, New York 3, N.Y.
Empire Artist's Materials, 135 East 60th St., New York 22, N.Y.
Gla-son Paint Products, Inc., 59 West 56th St., New York 19, N.Y.
E. P. Lynch, Inc., 92 Weybosset St., Providence, R.I.
The Stone Co., Inc., 19-21 Elm St., Danbury, Conn.
Brenner's Paint Shop, 8 Samoset St., Plymouth, Mass.
The Paint Shop, 292 Centre St., Newton, Mass.
The Dauber Shop, 18 Mica Lane, Wellesley Hills 82, Mass.
Centre Hardware, 5 South Main St., Uxbridge, Mass.

The following are firms specializing in tinware and woodenware.

Colonial Handcraft Trays, New Market, Virginia.
Crafts Mfg. Co., Lunenburg, Mass.
Village Tin Shop, 1030 Main St., Hingham, Mass.
S. & B. Wood Specialties, 74 La Salle St., East Longmeadow, Mass.
The Country Loft, Newfields, New Hampshire.
The Kitchen Tinshop, 23 School St., Lisbon, New Hampshire.
Hoitt & Wentworth, 559 Central Avenue, Dover, New Hampshire.

3 Preparation of Tin for Decoration

This chapter and the next one deal with the preparation of actual objects for decoration. The beginning student, however, need not spend time on them, but may turn straight on to Chapters 6 to 10 which impart the techniques of decoration. When practice and skill have been acquired in these techniques, the time has come for trays and other articles to be prepared for decoration, and this and the next chapter should receive due attention.

1 Removing Old Paint or Varnish

The work of preparing a surface for decoration is as important as the decoration itself. The first step is to remove all old paint or varnish, for which purpose any good brand of paint and varnish remover will do. To reduce the chance of inhaling the fumes, work with the windows open. Read and follow the directions on the can, and have plenty of rags and old newspapers close at hand.

2 Removing Rust

In its initial stages rust is invisible to the naked eye, and therefore all tinware should be treated for rust whether it is observed or not. For this purpose, Deoxidine #624 is recommended. Deoxidine not only removes rust, but also cleanses the metal and minutely etches the surface, with the result that paint will adhere better. Proceed as follows.

(a) Dilute one part of Deoxidine with three parts of cold water, mixing only enough for the job in hand. Apply the solution to the tin surface with a paint brush, and leave it on for 5 minutes.

(b) Rub the surface with steel wool, and then apply the solution again for 5 minutes. Rub again with steel wool.

(c) Rinse the article thoroughly in cold water, and dry it well. The yellowish color that may appear is not rust.

(d) Apply the primer paint without delay once the article is completely dry.

If the tray or other article is badly rusted, several applications of Deoxidine solution may be necessary. This is particularly true of old articles into which the rust has eaten deeply. In restoration work, when as much as possible of the original paint is to be retained, it is safe to apply Deoxidine to the rusted parts, as it will not harm the surrounding paint.

3 *Before Painting a Surface*

The painting of a surface falls into two main parts, primer painting and flat background painting, which are described in turn in sections 4 and 5 which follow. But before applying any coat of paint, whether primer or background color, it is essential to note these three directions:

(a) Stir the can of paint carefully with a stick until the contents are thoroughly mixed. Avoid slopping the paint over the rim of the can, and do not stop stirring until it is *completely* mixed. It may take 10 minutes.

(b) Dust off the surface with a lintless cloth, making sure no particle of dust remains. Just before applying the paint, rub the palm of your hand over the surface, picking up any minute particles in the corners.

(c) Never paint a second coat until the first one is at least 24 hours old, and unless it feels completely and thoroughly dry. Wait if it feels the least bit sticky, even if you have to wait a week because of bad weather.

4 *Primer Painting*

A tin surface must always be given one or two coats of primer paint before the background color is applied, or the latter will not adhere properly. Any color will do for this primer. The primer paint should be applied *immediately* after the tin surface has been treated for rust. Spread plenty of newspapers on a table or other working surface, and be sure the paint has been thoroughly mixed.

In applying the primer to a tray, first paint the underside of the flange or border, leaving the central surface untouched. Then turn the tray over, and holding it balanced on your left hand, paint first the top side of the flange, and afterwards the *floor* of the tray, using long strokes the full length of the tray floor.

Don't flood the tray with primer, but use just enough to cover the surface. Don't go back to retouch any of it. Paint it, and leave it. Last of all, hold the tray high and check the underside for any drippings. Finally, set the tray down on a tin can placed on a spread newspaper, and let it dry for 24 hours. When applying the second coat, paint the floor of the tray in the opposite direction. After the second coat is thoroughly dry, sandpaper it to remove any tiny "pinheads."

The bottom of the tray is left unpainted until the rest of the tray is completely finished, including its decoration and the finishing coats of varnish. Then the bottom is rubbed off with turpentine and is given two coats of flat black paint.

5 *Flat Background Painting*

A properly painted background, whether black or any other color, should be a completely flat or dull surface, feeling smooth and free from

10

ridges when the hand is run over it. If you can feel any ridges, your paint was not sufficiently thinned with turpentine. To rectify this by sandpapering the surface until it is smooth may take a great deal of time and hard work; therefore apply the paint correctly in the first place and you will save yourself trouble later on. With this preliminary word of caution in mind, the following directions should be carefully studied and followed.

The paint should be thinned with enough turpentine to make a very watery mixture. Usually there is not enough room in a fresh can of paint for the necessary amount of turpentine to thin the paint properly. Procure a small empty jar, and pour into it about a quarter of an inch of turpentine. After stirring the can of black paint until it is thoroughly mixed, dip out one or two brushfuls, and add them to the turpentine in the jar. Mix with the brush. The resulting mixture should be quite thin and watery.

After dusting the surface, apply the thinned black just as you did the primer coat. Because of the thinness of the paint, the first coat will not completely hide a white undercoat, but do not go back to touch up. Leave it, and let it dry for 24 hours at least. Then apply the second coat. There should be at least three coats; four are preferred. In each case, paint the floor of the tray in the opposite direction to the previous coat, so as to contribute to an even result.

Sandpaper the last coat *very lightly* with a square inch or so of fine sandpaper. A little piece of sandpaper can be controlled better than a large one, and there is less likelihood of using too heavy a hand. Sandpaper chiefly the floor of the tray, avoiding the edges and other "vulnerable" parts, such as the bumps on a chippendale tray.

Allow the paint to harden for at least a week before doing a design on it. A longer period of waiting, such as a month, can be recommended, especially when a freehand gold or gold leaf design is to be applied.

6   Tin Boxes

Paint only the outside of a tin box. The inside is not usually painted, but is merely oiled from time to time to keep it from rusting.

7   "Mass Production"

Mass production in the usual sense of the term is not applicable to American antique decoration! But I use the expression to convey to learners the value of the economical use of time and effort. Practically never do I paint only one object at a time. By a little planning ahead you can generally arrange to carry several articles through the routine from Deoxidine to background painting. Then you can please yourself when you want to decorate them. Similarly, when the time comes to apply the finishing coats of varnish, it is very economical to wait until you have several pieces to do.

11

4   Preparation of Wood for Decoration

Old Wood

The re-decoration of old chairs, boxes, chests, cupboards, tables, etc., is one of the most satisfying ways of using American antique decoration techniques. Countless plain pieces have thus been converted into things of beauty; some which were thrown out with the rubbish have been rescued and turned into objects of admiration and envy.

The steps in the preparation of old wood for decoration are these:

(a) Remove the old paint or varnish as described in section 1, Chapter 3.

(b) Fill in all holes and cracks with plastic wood. Let it dry.

(c) Obtain a smooth surface by sandpapering the flat parts, and by rubbing the turned parts and any carving with steel wool.

(d) Apply three or four thin coats of flat background paint as described in section 5, Chapter 3.

(e) Again use the sandpaper and steel wool, but this time only *very lightly*, and keeping well away from all edges. To rub the painted edges would entirely remove the paint from them.

New Wood

In the case of new wood, the process of preparation is as follows:

(a) Sandpaper well, first using fairly coarse paper, and then the finer kind. Use steel wool on the turned parts and carving.

(b) Fill in crevices with plastic wood. When it is dry, sandpaper again.

(c) Apply a coat of shellac to seal the wood. Let it dry for 24 hours.

(d) Sandpaper again.

(e) Apply three or four coats of thin background paint in the way previously described (section 5, Chapter 3).

(f) Sandpaper very lightly, avoiding rubbing the edges.

Graining

A simple grained background was sometimes used on painted furniture, in order to imitate expensive woods. Occasionally it was used on boxes. The graining was generally done over a dull red painted background, or over a stained walnut one. There is more than one method of graining. The following is the one which I personally prefer.

First, apply the dull red background color in the usual three or four

12

thin coats of flat paint as described in Chapter 3. The color may be bought as Venetian Red or obtained by mixing Brown with Vermilion.

When the background color is thoroughly dry, apply a coat of thin black paint. The graining effect is done lengthwise along the wood and is achieved by immediately pulling a crumpled piece of old muslin across the wet surface. In the case of a large piece of furniture, do the graining in suitable sections. Have several small pieces of muslin on hand. When one piece becomes too full of paint, take a fresh piece. Let the work dry for 24 hours.

On a stenciled chair, the main slat is not grained, but is painted black.

5 Mixing Colors

Background Colors

For these use good-quality, flat indoor paints. Do not use glossy enamels. Pratt & Lambert's Sta Blac *Flat* Enamel gives an excellent dull black surface when it is sufficiently thinned with turpentine. Always remember to mix paint thoroughly before using.

Most of our other background colors have to be obtained by mixing, and for this work it is necessary to save small screw-top jars, such as cold-cream jars. It is important when mixing a color to be sure there is enough left over for touching up after the decoration has been completed, and the jars serve to keep the colors fresh.

In mixing for a background color, mix the pigments first, and then add the turpentine to get the proper watery consistency. For this reason, mix a relatively small quantity of the thick color, allowing for the fact that you will have a much larger quantity after the turpentine has been added.

Antique Black

To obtain this, put a little flat black in a clean jar, adding to it some Raw Umber and White. The best way to go about this is to squeeze a little of each of the two last-named colors on to an old saucer, and to dissolve them by mixing in some of the black with a showcard brush. When no lumps remain, add the mixture to the jar of flat black, and stir well with a small stick. Test the color on a piece of paper, using the showcard brush. Keep mixing and adding until the proper shade has been reached. Antique black is really off-black, that is, a very dark, soft, charcoal color. It is very effective with country patterns.

Light Colors

Use flat white paint as a base for all light colors, adding Japan or oil colors to get the desired color. Always allow for the darkening effect of the finishing coats of varnish and, of course, for any antiquing you may intend to do. Among the most used light background colors are these:

Off-white: White with a little Raw Umber added.
Cream: White with a little Yellow Ochre added.
Pale antique yellow: White, Japan Yellow, and Raw Umber.
Pale apple green: White, Japan Yellow, Raw Umber, and a touch of Prussian Blue.

14

Medium Colors

Use the nearest color flat paint, and tone with tube colors, as for example:

Venetian red: Vermilion, Burnt Umber, and White.
Olive green: Green, Burnt Umber, and Yellow Ochre.

Asphaltum

A background which falls into a class by itself is "asphaltum," as we call a mixture of asphaltum or asphalt and varnish. It is a semi-transparent background used over bright tin and is difficult to apply satisfactorily. Old examples invariably show more or less streakiness, and therefore beginners need not be unduly discouraged by the results of their first attempts.

If the tin has darkened with age or use, no longer presenting a uniformly shiny surface, apply a coat of clear varnish. When this is tacky, apply aluminum or chrome powder with a velvet finger, and then burnish it by applying extra pressure. This will give a simulated shiny tin surface. Wait 24 hours. Then wash off all loose powder under running cold water, pat the surface thoroughly dry with a lintless cloth, and apply a coat of varnish to protect the surface. Let it dry for another 24 hours.

Asphalt can be bought in a tube. It should be mixed in a saucer with varnish, to which is added a little each of Alizarin Crimson and of Burnt Umber. The quantity used of these oil colors determines the color of the asphaltum, and the quantity of varnish determines its transparency.

Apply the mixture with a varnish brush, working quickly. Do not go back and repaint any part of it. If you have enough of the mixture on your brush as you apply it, the streakiness will more or less disappear when the asphaltum settles. Use discarded tin cans to experiment with in applying the mixture, and to find out what shade of background you like best. Asphaltum must be allowed to dry for at least a week.

Color Key for Painted Patterns

The following are more or less standard colors, ones that recur again and again in American antique designs. Here they are arranged in convenient groups: first the reds, then the greens, then the blues, and so on. The method by which the different shades are obtained is added. Rarely do we use bright color fresh from the tube. Indeed, with the exception of Vermilion, all the bright colors must be toned down by the addition of Yellow Ochre or one of the browns in order to obtain those beautiful, soft, antique shades of color that are such a joy to live with. Mix the colors with the showcard brush, using varnish as the medium. Of course, the colors must be mixed completely, so that no lumps of pigment remain.

15

Prefixed to each color is the letter or letters by which it is indicated in the black-and-white drawings in this book.

V	bright red	Japan Vermilion.
S	salmon pink	Japan Vermilion, Yellow Ochre, and a touch of White.
A	dark red overtone	Alizarin Crimson, with a touch of Burnt Umber and enough varnish to make a semi-transparent rich dark red.
G	country green	Japan Green, with a touch of Burnt Umber.
LG	light country green	Japan Green with a little Japan Yellow, and a touch of Burnt Umber.
DG	dark country green	Japan Green, a touch of Raw Umber and Prussian Blue.
YG	yellow green	Japan Yellow, a little Japan Green, and a touch of Raw Umber.
B	medium blue	Prussian Blue, with a little Raw Umber and White.
LB	light blue	White with a little Prussian Blue and Raw Umber.
DB	dark blue	Prussian Blue, with Raw Umber and a touch of White.
RU	dark brown	Raw Umber.
BU	medium brown	Burnt Umber.
BS	reddish brown	Burnt Sienna.
Y	mustard yellow	Japan Yellow, with Burnt Umber added a little at a time until you get the color you want. For a greenish mustard, use Raw Umber. For an orange mustard, use Burnt Sienna.
W	off white	White with a touch of Raw Umber. For white overtones, use enough varnish to make the mixture semi-transparent.

6 Country Painting

The first step towards proficiency in country painting is to learn its typical brush strokes. Take a double sheet of newspaper and fold it into eighths so as to make a handy "palette." Newspaper is used because it has the advantage of absorbing superfluous oil in the paint. Next you will need the following: a small bottle cap filled with varnish; a tube of Japan Vermilion; a square-tipped show card brush for mixing; a square-tipped camel's-hair quill brush for painting; some tracing paper; a small jar half full of Carbona Cleaning Fluid for cleaning brushes. With these items you can proceed to practice the brush strokes.

Place a piece of tracing paper over Plate 1. Squeeze out a little color on the newspaper, and dipping out some varnish with the showcard brush, mix it with a small quantity of color. The mixture should contain enough varnish to make it manageable, and yet it must not be so thin that it spreads once it has been painted.

Take up the quill brush and dip it into the paint mixture, loading the brush its full length, not just the tip of it. Now hold the brush as illustrated in Plate 1. Hold it as vertically as possible, with the wrist off the ground, and the hand resting lightly on the tip of the little finger. Rest the forearm on the table edge.

Paint the broad stripe as seen through the tracing paper, and observe how the brush flattens out to a knife-edge now that it is lowered. Next, slowly raising the brush, pull it off to one side, using the knife-edge to end the stroke on a hairline.

Now go on to paint the rows of brush strokes in the illustration, starting at the broad end of each stroke, and gradually raising the brush to end on a hairline. Paint each stroke slowly and deliberately. If your stroke finishes too thick, either you had too much paint mixture on the brush or you did not raise the brush enough. Too much paint on the brush may also cause the strokes to spread a few minutes after you have painted them.

Except for very small strokes, reload the brush for each stroke, always reloading to its full length. With practice you will learn to load the brush instinctively with just the right amount of paint for the size of stroke you desire.

For a stroke that starts on a point and ends on a point, flatten the brush on the newspaper palette, and then holding the brush high, begin the stroke; lower the brush to do the broad part of the stroke, and finally lift it to complete the stroke. For a thin line or vein, flatten the brush on

LG

V

L

V

Y→

TEA CADDY

PLATE 1 PRACTICE YOUR BRUSH STROKES

the newspaper and then paint with the knifelike edge. For a dot, round the brush on the newspaper, and then holding the brush high, paint the dot with the end of the brush.

Whenever the paint begins to thicken, clean the brush in Carbona. Squeeze out a little fresh paint, and mix with varnish on another part of the newspaper.

Don't hesitate to turn your work round to any convenient angle that suits the particular stroke you are doing; turn the work upside down if necessary. A good stroke is the result of patience and practice. By practicing half an hour every day for a week or two you should have a fair command of the brush.

Tea Caddy Pattern on Plate 1

To make a copy of this pattern, cut a piece of frosted acetate large enough for the design, and attach it at three corners to a piece of thin cardboard, using for the purpose small pieces of decorator's tape. Slip this contrivance into the book in the manner shown in the drawing in the lower left-hand corner of Plate 1, which will have the effect of bringing the tea caddy pattern under the acetate. By painting the pattern directly on the acetate you will get not only a color record of it, but also valuable practice. The stages are these:

1. On a newspaper palette squeeze out a little Japan Vermilion. Using the showcard brush, dip several brushfuls of varnish out of the bottle cap, and mix them with a small quantity of the color. Paint the three large "flowers" marked V, disregarding the overtone strokes. The paint should be opaque, but yet contain sufficient varnish for it to dry smooth and flat. Clean the brush by wiping off the excess paint on a rag, and then dipping it in Carbona.

2. Squeeze out a little Japan Green and a tiny bit of Burnt Umber. With the showcard brush mix some Green, adding a speck of Burnt Umber to tone down the Green a little. With this "country green" mixture, paint those "leaves" which are shown black in the illustration, using your quill brush for this purpose.

3. Squeeze out a little Japan Yellow and add a touch of it to the green mixture, making a much lighter and yellower green. With this mixture, paint the leaves, which are shown white in the illustration.

4. Clean the showcard brush, and use it to mix a little Yellow with a touch of Burnt Umber. With the cleaned camel's-hair quill brush, paint the dots. Remove the cardboard and acetate from the book, and set it aside to dry for 24 hours.

5. To paint the shaded and the dotted overtones on the vermilion flowers, do not put the acetate back over the illustration. These are done by eye, using the illustration as a guide. On a clean newspaper palette mix

19

PLATE 2   STRAWBERRY CHAIR: YELLOW BACKGROUND

several brushfuls of varnish with some Alizarin Crimson and a touch of Burnt Umber, making a rich, dark, semi-transparent red. With this mixture, and using the quill brush, paint the dotted overtone strokes on the flowers. Use only one stroke for each overtone. If you make a mistake, wipe it off with a clean cloth at once, before it has time to set.

6. For the shaded overtone strokes in the illustration, mix some varnish with a little White and add a touch of Raw Umber to make a semi-transparent white overtone. When this is painted on the vermilion flower, it will take on a faintly pinkish tone. Set aside to dry for 24 hours.

Strawberry Chair on Plate 2

To make a copy of this pattern, cut a piece of frosted acetate and place it over the illustration, as described above for the tea caddy pattern. Proceed as follows:

1. On a newspaper palette mix some varnish and Japan Vermilion, and paint the whole area of the two strawberry shapes, covering the overlapping leaves, the shading, and the seed marks. Remove the acetate from the book and let it dry for 24 hours.

2. On either side of each strawberry are dotted areas which are done in semi-transparent dark red, made by mixing some Alizarin Crimson with varnish and adding a touch of Burnt Umber. With one or two strokes of the showcard brush, apply this mixture to the berries, taking care not to go over the edges, as it would show on any pale background color. Don't fuss over it. Do it once and leave it.

Immediately take a camel's-hair quill brush, dip it in the varnish, and wipe off some of the varnish on the newspaper palette, at the same time flattening the brush. Now, with one stroke, draw the flattened brush along the inner edge of the dark red overtone, with the brush partly on the red and partly off. This will blend and soften the edge of the dark red, giving the berry a softly shaded look.

If you use too much varnish on the blending brush, it will spread and disturb the smooth appearance of the dark red. Practice will enable you to know just how much to use each time.

3. Twenty-four hours later, mix some Japan Green with a touch of Burnt Umber, and paint all the leaves and brush strokes which are black in the illustration. Wait 24 hours.

4. Mix some Japan Yellow with a touch of Raw Umber, and using enough varnish to make the mixture slightly transparent, paint the seeds on the berries and the veins in the leaves.

5. With Japan Black, paint the curlicues, using a fine quill brush.

To Decorate a Chair

Before proceeding to decorate a chair with this pattern, you should study the instructions as to preparation and background color which are given in Chapters 4 and 5. The pattern was taken from a chair that was painted a pale antique yellow. This color can be made by mixing White with Japan Yellow, adding a little Raw Umber, and thinning with turpentine to a very watery consistency. Apply three or four coats.

Striping

See Chapter 14 as to the general method of striping. The striping on the chair was done in two colors. The broad stripe, about ⅛ inch wide, running around the main slat and the seat, was in a transparent dark red, made by mixing Alizarin Crimson and a touch of Burnt Umber. This was also used to accent some of the turnings. See Plate 19. The fine striping on the side back posts, the seat (just inside the red stripe), the smaller slat, and on some of the turnings, was done in country green to match the leaves, and was about $\frac{1}{16}$ inch wide.

Position of Chair

The most convenient way to decorate a chair is to lay it on its back on a table, and to work upside down. Turn the pattern you are copying upside down too. This method of procedure applies to stenciling as well as to freehand painting.

I STENCILED BOSTON ROCKER—19½″ long

II STENCILED VILLAGE SCENE—15″ long

III STENCILED HITCHCOCK-TYPE CHAIR PATTERN—14″ long

IV STENCILED BREAD TRAY—12¾″ long

V STENCILED RECTANGULAR TRAY—15″ × 20″

VI STENCILED CHAIR PATTERN A—13″ long

VII STENCILED CHAIR PATTERN B—12½″ long

VIII STENCILED WATERING CAN AND CANDLE HOLDER

IX   STENCILING

X STRAWBERRY CHAIR PATTERN—11″ long and
FREEHAND BRONZE CHAIR—13″ long

XI GOLD LEAF TRAY—9″ × 12″

7 Freehand Bronze

Freehand bronze painting is the term used to describe a method of applying various metal powders to a pattern without the use of a stencil. The word "bronze," when used in this connection, covers a large variety of metal powders which give the effect of gold and silver as well as bronze. It was, no doubt, in imitation of the splendid but expensive process of gold leaf decoration that "gold" metal powder was first used, and the use of other metallic colors naturally followed.

For this work an absolutely dry background of flat paint is essential; otherwise the loose bronze powders will stick to the background. The design is painted freehand with a varnish mixture, and when it is tacky it is burnished or shaded with the metal powders.

To Copy a Tray Border

A good way to learn freehand bronze is to copy on to a sheet of frosted acetate the simple tray border shown at the top of Plate 3. Proceed as follows:

1. Place the acetate over the design.

2. On a newspaper palette, and using the ox-hair brush, mix some Japan Vermilion with a little varnish. Using the quill brush, begin by painting the first flower, then its three large leaves, and then its smaller leaves. Paint the overall surface of the flower, going over all the details and shaded areas. Proceed to the other flower and its leaves in the same order. Apply the paint evenly, avoid leaving any overly wet places, and do not go back and repaint any part. Paint it and leave it. Your work should present a flat, even surface. In working along, keep a watch on the areas already painted, and, as they begin to dry, apply pale gold powder with a velvet finger, using a small circular motion and a very light touch. Continue in this way, painting and applying the powder to the drying areas.

The secret of success is to apply the powder at just the right stage of dryness. If you do it too soon, the surface of the paint will be roughened and some of the hairs of the velvet will stick to it. If you wait too long, the surface will be too dry for the powder to stick. The flowers and large leaves will take longer to reach the proper stage than the smaller parts of the design.

When you have finished applying the last of the gold powder, lay the pattern aside to dry for 24 hours.

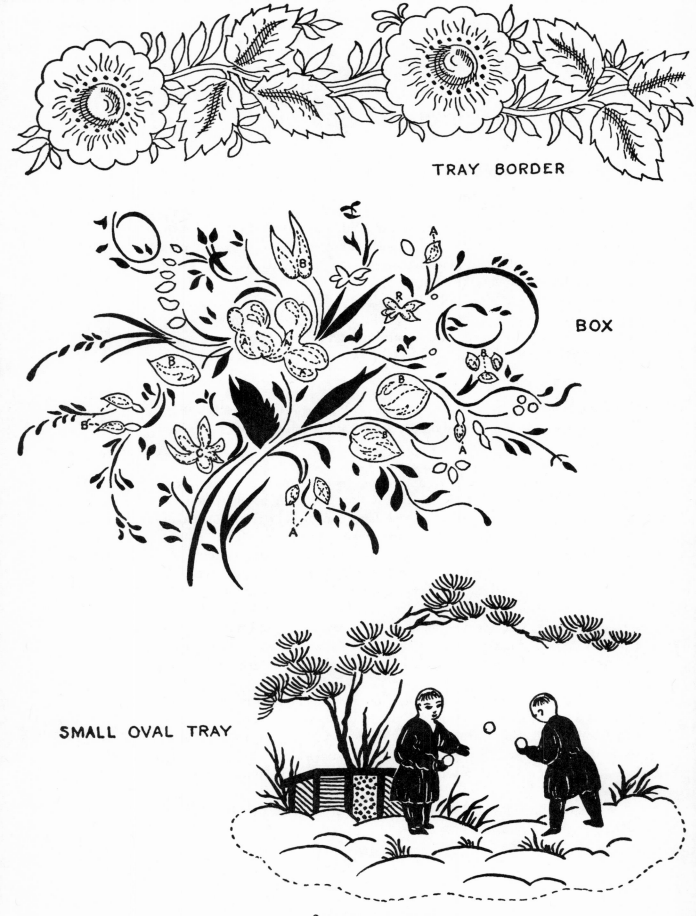

TRAY BORDER

BOX

SMALL OVAL TRAY

PLATE 3   FREEHAND BRONZE

3. Next day, gently wipe off the excess gold powder with a cloth. Then draw the details with pen and ink. Allow half an hour for drying.

4. Apply Burnt Umber shading on the areas marked with fine parallel lines. A thin mixture of varnish and Burnt Umber is used. Allow the work 24 hours to dry.

Excess Bronze Powder

It is sometimes difficult, after the 24-hour drying period, to wipe off the excess powder from a tray or other object. In the case of a metal object, such as a tray, the excess can be washed off by running cold water over it. If you are working on an article made of wood, it is better to wipe it well with a damp sponge, after which the surface may be dried by patting it with a linen towel. If powder still remains, paint it out with the original background paint.

The finer bronze powders, such as the lining powders, tend to stick in the wrong places if the opportunity is given them. They give a more beautiful surface than the coarser powders, but need to be used with the greatest care. If we bring a little patience and perseverance to this work, the most gratifying results will be attained.

To Copy the Box Pattern

1. Put a sheet of frosted acetate over this pattern in Plate 3. Using a quill brush, paint in all the black parts with a mixture of Japan Vermilion and varnish. When the work is tacky, apply the gold powder. Let it dry for 24 hours.

2. Wipe off the excess gold powder. Paint the white areas with a mixture of Titanium White, a touch of Raw Umber, and a little varnish. Allow 24 hours to dry.

3. The dotted lines in the design indicate areas of transparent colored overtones, which are applied with one or two strokes of the quill brush. Do not fuss over this—do it and leave it. If the first application is not right, instantly wipe it off with a soft cloth, and do it again.

The red (marked with an A) is made of varnish mixed with a little Alizarin Crimson and a touch of Burnt Umber. The blue (B) is a similar mixture of varnish with a little Prussian Blue and Raw Umber. The chartreuse green (C) is obtained with Indian Yellow and a touch of Prussian Blue.

To Copy the Small Chinese Tray

1. Put a sheet of frosted acetate over this pattern in Plate 3. With Japan Vermilion paint in the black parts excepting the details on the heads. When tacky, apply the gold powder. Wait 24 hours.

2. Wipe off excess powder. Paint in the heads with a pale flesh color

25

obtained by mixing White with a little Indian Yellow and a touch of Alizarin Crimson. While the work is still wet, work in a little more crimson on the faces. By adding still more crimson to the flesh color, make a deep rose, and use it to paint in the three balls. Wait 24 hours.

3. Give the entire sheet of acetate a coat of varnish, and when it is almost dry, cloud in a little pale gold powder to indicate faintly the ground. Wait 24 hours.

4. With pen and ink, draw in the faces and hair, and the details of the clothes. This is done after the application of the varnish, so that if any mistakes are made they can easily be erased without affecting the other parts of the design.

8 Stenciling

Stenciling is done on a partly dry, varnished surface, by applying bronze powders through a stencil. Black is the usual and typical background color, as this gives depth and roundness to the shaded leaves, fruits, flowers, etc. When stenciling is found on light-colored chairs (such as an apple green or a salmon pink), the main slat carrying the stenciled design is painted black.

Tracing Stencils

Our stencils are made out of architect's tracing linen, which is semi-transparent, enabling the design to be traced directly on it. The tracing is done on the dull side of the cloth by means of a crow-quill pen and black drawing ink. In Plate 5 are shown the units for an old Boston Rocker pattern, the black parts being the areas that are to be cut out.

In tracing each unit on linen, allow an inch of linen around the unit. The larger units should be on separate pieces of linen, but the smaller ones may be traced two on a piece so long as care is taken to allow an inch of space in between. For example, figures 5 and 6 of Plate 5 may both

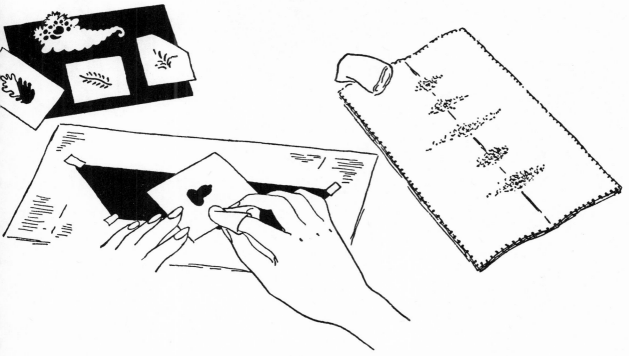

PLATE 4 STENCILING WITH BRONZE POWDERS

27

PALEGOLD & FIRE
2

1
PALEGOLD

7

5 FIRE 6

4 & 4A
PALEGOLD

PALEGOLD
3

8 END PIECE

LINEN

SEAT FRONT
PALEGOLD

PALEGOLD EDGE

PLATE 5   STENCILED BOSTON ROCKER

be traced on one piece of linen but with an inch of linen between them and, of course, one inch of linen all around the outside of them.

Note that in the case of figure 4 *two* stencils are required, one for the leaf and one for the veining.

A photograph of the finished pattern is shown in Photo. I between pp. 22-23, where the various units can be seen in their correct relative positions. Notice that figure 8 is different from the others in that, instead of being cut out, the unit is a piece of linen with a cut-off edge. Hence there is no one-inch margin to consider.

Cutting Stencils

It is important to have the proper scissors (see page 5), a comfortable chair, and a good light over your shoulder. Be comfortable and be relaxed. A black cloth on your lap will make it easier to see the job and at the same time will serve to catch the scraps that fall.

During the actual cutting, take care not to stretch the edges of the linen. Do not pierce the cloth directly on the line, but rather inside it. For a stem running to pointed ends, pierce the cloth in the middle, and cut towards the point. A tiny dot is cut by piercing the linen with the point of the scissors, and then taking five or six tiny cuts around, using only the very points of the scissors. In a unit composed of many pieces, such as figure 7, cut the smallest pieces first, gradually working up to the largest ones last. When the stencils have all been cut, number the pieces in ink to correspond with the numbers of the figures in Plate 5, and write on each the color of bronze powder which is to be used with it.

Black Paper

The pattern should be stenciled on black paper before doing it on a rocker. Cut a piece of black paper about 20 by 5 inches, and tack this to a larger piece of clean newspaper, using tiny bits of masking tape at the corners. A beginner would do well to practice stenciling a pattern several times on black paper, as it is much easier to throw away a mistake on paper than to clean off and re-do a black surface on a piece of furniture.

Varnishing

Carefully dust off the surface to be varnished, and assemble all the necessary equipment before opening the varnish can. You will need plenty of newspapers to spread down, the varnish brush, a paint rag, and the brush bath. The latter is a jar half full of Energine.

Do not shake or stir the can of varnish. Flick your brush to get rid of any loose hairs or dust particles. Dip the hairs of the brush about one half their length into the varnish, and holding one end of the black paper down with the left hand, begin to apply the varnish. Press the brush down all the way, and use long strokes the full length of the paper. Work with the light falling across the paper so you can see that every bit of surface is being covered. Work quickly and surely, taking more varnish only as you need it, but never flooding the surface. Now hold the black paper down at the top, and without taking any more varnish, go over the surface in the crosswise direction, thus making sure that there is an even distribution of varnish.

If you have used too much varnish and the surface seems very wet, wipe the brush off on some clean newspaper and then quickly pick up the excess varnish. Last of all, with a very light touch, and using only the tip of the brush, pick up any tiny bubbles on the surface. Set the paper aside to dry in a dust-free place. Follow the same procedure when you come to varnish a tray or a chair slat.

The weather and the amount of varnish used will determine how long it will take for the varnished surface to reach the proper tacky stage for stenciling. It generally takes about 45 minutes to an hour, but on a wet day it would take longer. The proper tacky stage is reached when the surface is sticky to the touch, but yet the fingertip leaves no mark on the surface.

Stenciling

While the varnish is drying, assemble your stencils, and check them to be sure you have all of them. Set up your mohair palette with tiny mounds of palegold and fire powders, as illustrated in Plate 4. Wrap the velvet "finger" (see page 27) around your forefinger as shown in the illustration, drawing the folds tightly to the back of the finger, and holding it in place with the third finger. The tiny working surface of velvet on your fingertip should be smooth, and only about one quarter of an inch in diameter. If your finger happens to be larger than that, stencil with the side of the fingertip.

When the black paper has reached the proper tacky stage, begin to stencil by placing stencil 1 in position on the black paper, using Photo. I between pp. 22-23 as your guide. With the velvet "finger" pick up so little palegold that it is barely visible, and then with a light *circular* touch apply the powder around the outer edges of the leaves where they are brightest, taking up more powder as needed. After the brightest parts are stenciled, go over them with a little more pressure to burnish them, and then go lightly over the rest of the unit to achieve a shaded and rounded effect. Lift the stencil.

If you pick up too much powder on the velvet, just tap it on a clean part of the mohair, and the high pile will take it off instantly. If you apply too much powder to the black surface, there is no way of taking it up again; hence work cautiously.

30

Place stencil 2 in position and apply the palegold brightly at the very top of the pineapple. Then with a clean part of the velvet pick up some fire powder and go back over the palegold, working on down the fruit and fading out to *deep black* before you reach the leaves of stencil 1. It is the quick transition from very bright gold shading to fire and then to deep black that gives roundness to the fruit. Next, stencil 3 is done in palegold, very bright at the outer edges, fading quickly to black before you get to the pineapple.

Still referring to Photograph I for guidance, do stencil 4 in palegold, very bright around the edges of the leaf, leaving the center black; after which the veins are done in palegold. Then flower stencil 5 is done in fire, one at a time, followed by stencil 6, also in fire. Stencil 7 is then added, one on either side. Last of all, stencil 8 is carried out on the ends of the slat. The stencil is used for one end, after which it is cleaned on both sides with Carbona, and then reversed to stencil the other end. Palegold is used for both 7 and 8.

Always remember when stenciling to apply the powder with a light circular motion of the velvet. Do not dab it on. Also, after the brightest parts have been stenciled, go over them again with a little more pressure to burnish them.

When you have finished stenciling a pattern, immediately clean the stencils on both sides with Energine or Carbona, using a soft cotton cloth. They dry in a few minutes. Let the stenciled pattern dry for 24 hours.

9 Floating Color

The rose on the Queen Anne style tray, (Photo. XVIII between pp. 38-39) is a typical floating color rose. It is done in three stages, each stage being allowed to dry thoroughly before the next one is painted. The characteristic subtle blending of color is produced by floating the color on in the second stage. For this process, you will need a small bottle of "slow varnish," which is composed of one part linseed oil and two parts varnish. This you can mix yourself. Be sure to label the bottle, so as not to confuse it with ordinary varnish.

Incidentally, do not attempt to do floating color work until you have had a fair amount of practice in country painting.

To copy the Queen Anne tray center, slip a piece of frosted acetate over the drawing in Plate 6. In the original pattern, the leaves and stems were all in gold leaf, the application of which will be dealt with in Chapter 10. Meanwhile, satisfactory results can be obtained by using palegold bronze powder as already described in Chapter 7 (Freehand Bronze). Proceed as follows:

1. On a newspaper palette, mix some varnish with a little Japan Vermilion, and paint the leaves and stems. First do the larger leaves, then the next larger, and so on, down to the thin stems. When the proper tacky stage has been reached, apply the palegold powder. Wait 24 hours.

2. Dust off the excess powder.

3. Disregarding all details, paint the overall area of flower A with a subdued orange, made by mixing Japan Vermilion, Yellow Ochre, and White. Using a creamy white, produced by mixing White with a little Raw Umber and Yellow Ochre, paint the overall shapes of the other two large flowers (B and C), the bluebells (D), and the small flowers and buds. Remove the acetate from the book, and let it dry for 24 hours.

4. On a newspaper palette squeeze out a little Alizarin Crimson, Burnt Umber, Prussian Blue, Raw Umber, and Indian Yellow. Dust off the surface of the pattern.

For flower A, dip the showcard brush into the bottle of slow varnish, and apply a coat of the mixture over the entire flower, but just short of the outer edge all round, since the varnish will spread a little of its own accord. Do not flood it on, but use just enough to cover the area comfortably.

Wipe off your brush on a rag to get rid of most of the slow varnish, and pick up a little *dry* Alizarin Crimson and a speck of Burnt Umber on the tip of the flattened brush. With a light touch, brush in the red on the shaded (broken-line) areas of flower A, adding a bit more pigment just

PLATE 6 CENTER FOR "QUEEN ANNE" TRAY

under the stamens. Work quickly. Do not fuss over the streaks. After a few minutes of standing, the transparent color should have blended in with the slow varnish.

5. Clean the brush, and apply a coat of slow varnish to the rose C. Wipe the brush on a rag, and brush a little Indian Yellow all over the flower until you have a smooth transparent yellow tone. Then pick up a speck of Alizarin Crimson plus Burnt Umber, and lightly brush this pinky color under the "cup" of the rose, here and there around the edges, and also in the "heart" of the flower. Pick up a little more pigment, and darken the areas under the cup and in the heart of the rose.

6. With a clean brush, apply slow varnish to the bluebells D, treating both groups as units. Wipe off the brush on a rag. Pick up a speck of Prussian Blue and a tiny speck of Raw Umber, and apply a transparent deep blue to the lower third of the flowers. Using an even lighter touch than before, continue by fading the color off to a paler and paler blue, and finally to nothing, letting the white underpainting show at the top end of the bells. This completes the floating color on this pattern.

Note that anything with slow varnish in it needs at least a week to dry. It is not dry until every hint of stickiness is gone. However, after a day or two the other parts of the pattern may be painted.

7. With a thin mixture of Alizarin Crimson and Burnt Umber, apply a transparent red overtone to the flower B, leaving some of the white underpainting showing around the edges. Wipe off the brush a little, pick up a little *dry* Burnt Umber and work in a darker area at the center.

Paint the centers of the small white flowers with transparent red. Paint the veins of the leaves with Burnt Umber.

8. After the slow-varnish areas are thoroughly dry, dust off the surface. Using hardly any varnish at all, mix a little White with a touch of Raw Umber to get a thick off-white for accentuating the edges of the petals on the rose C, known as the "veiling." Paint one petal at a time, immediately taking a second brush with a little varnish on it, and using it to blend and soften the inner edge of each white stroke.

With a somewhat thinner mixture of off-white, paint the stamens on flower A and the centers of the small white flowers. For flower B, take the off-white brush, wipe it off a bit on the newspaper palette, and with this "dry" brush put in the strokes on the dark center.

Using a transparent green, made by mixing varnish with a little Indian Yellow and Prussian Blue, paint the shaded areas on the larger leaves and stems. Each time, apply the green with one or two strokes of the brush, and then taking a clean brush with a little varnish on it, immediately blend the edge of the color, so that it blends off nicely into the gold. Do not wait to do the blending until after all the green has been applied. Each patch of green must be blended off at once as it is painted. Let the work dry for 24 hours.

34

10 Gold Leaf

Gold leaf comes in two kinds of little booklets. In the one the leaves are mounted on tissue paper, and in the other they are unmounted. If you are learning to lay gold leaf without the personal guidance of a teacher, it is best to obtain the mounted kind, which is easier to handle than the other. Cut a piece of cardboard the size of the booklet, and lay the booklet on it, thus keeping the leaves flat, which generally facilitates handling.

Flat Background

As with freehand bronze painting, gold leaf work calls for an absolutely dry background of flat or dull paint; and preferably one that has been left a month to harden thoroughly.

To Prevent Sticking

Gold leaf has a tendency to stick in places where it is not wanted. To counteract this tendency, take some whiting, or Bon Ami cleansing powder, on a wet cloth, and go lightly over the surface. When it has dried, the resulting application is seen as a very faint film of white powder. Then transfer the design with magnesium carbonate, as described in Chapter 11. You can paint right over the white film. Later on, after the gold leaf has been applied and is dry, the film can be wiped off with a damp sponge.

Underpainting

The simplest way to start applying gold leaf is to lay a solid gold border, such as that on the tray in Photo. XI between pp. 22-23. For practice, place a sheet of frosted acetate over the section of this rectangular tray border shown in Plate 7. With a mixture of varnish and Yellow Ochre oil color, paint the background of the broad band on which the flowers, etc., appear, working quickly and evenly, with no areas wetter than others. Let the light fall across your work, so that you can be sure to cover every bit of surface as you go along. Guard against having an excess of varnish in the painting mixture, for that will make it spread. On the other hand, too much Yellow Ochre will result in a lumpy surface. With the same mixture, paint in the background for the three narrow gold stripes, namely, the one along the outer edge of the flange and the two inside the broad band which lie on the floor of the tray. Set the work aside until it is somewhat drier than is appropriate for stenciling, but is still tacky to the touch.

35

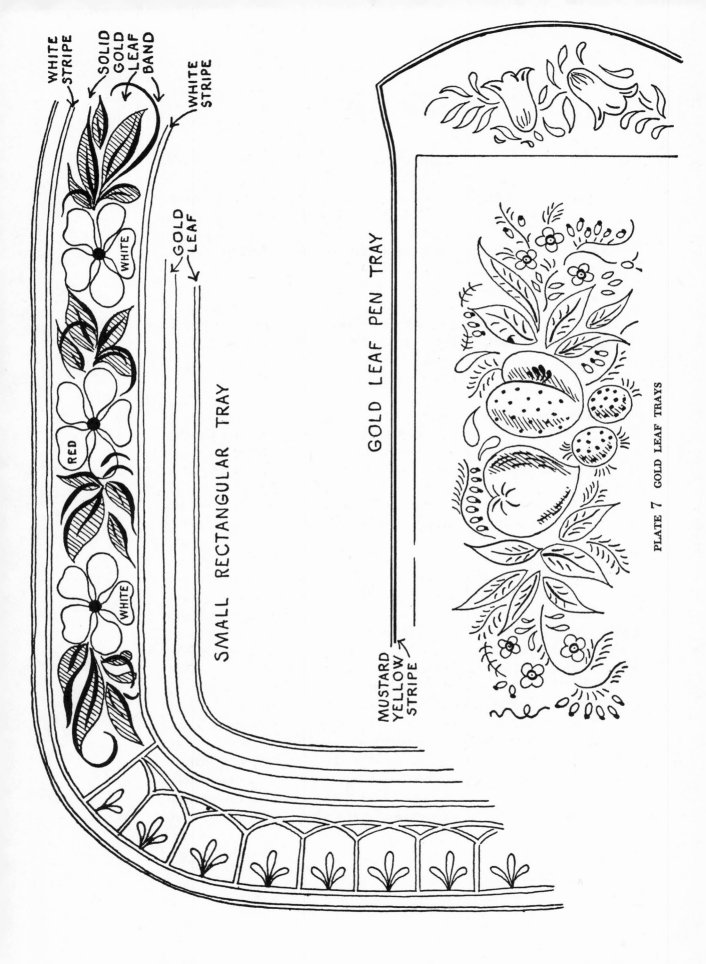

WHITE STRIPE

SOLID GOLD LEAF BAND

WHITE STRIPE

WHITE

GOLD LEAF

RED

WHITE

SMALL RECTANGULAR TRAY

GOLD LEAF PEN TRAY

MUSTARD YELLOW STRIPE

PLATE 7 GOLD LEAF TRAYS

Laying Gold Leaf

Note that, when laying gold leaf, it is important to see that the tissue paper does not touch the painted surface.

The proper tacky stage having been reached, pick up a mounted piece of gold leaf, holding it by the tissue paper with both hands, and with the gold side down. Hold it just above the painted border until you know exactly where you want it, and then lay it down on the tacky surface.

With a clean piece of velvet, press it down gently. Then lift up the tissue, and, with the remaining gold, go on to the next section, slightly overlapping the leaf as you apply it. Continue in this way until the gold on the tissue has been used up. With the fragments that may still remain, go back and touch up any small areas that, for one reason or another, did not get covered. A few hours after this part of the work is completed, gently remove all loose gold leaf with a clean piece of velvet. Let the work dry for 24 hours.

It would be a decided waste of gold leaf to practice the whole tray border on frosted acetate. By completing the border on an actual tray, you will get the best kind of practice.

Touching Up

After the gold leaf on a tray is 24 hours old, any places that are still without gold on them should be touched with clear varnish on a quill brush. But don't flood it on. Dip the brush in varnish, and wipe off a little on the newspaper palette before touching up. When the spots are tacky, which such tiny areas may become in a few minutes, lay the gold leaf. The whole job should then dry for a week.

Protective Coat of Varnish

Dust off the surface of the tray, making sure to remove not only dust but all stray bits of gold leaf as well. Then, before going on with the rest of the design, apply a coat of varnish to the tray as a protection for the gold leaf. After the varnish has dried for 24 hours, go over it very lightly with #000 steel wool, applying just enough pressure to take off the high gloss. This will give a good working surface for pen lines and any further painting.

Completion of the Small Rectangular Tray Pattern

Put a sheet of frosted acetate over Plate 7.

On a newspaper palette mix a little Japan Vermilion with varnish, and paint the center flower. With a mixture of off-white, paint the white flowers, and also the interlacing border design at the left. With a mixture of transparent deep green, made by mixing varnish with a little Indian Yellow and Prussian Blue, paint the shaded leaves. Wait 24 hours.

With Japan Black and a little varnish, paint the black accents on the leaves and the black flower centers. With a mixture of off-white, paint the stripes on either side of the gold leaf band area. Allow 24 hours to dry.

Gold Leaf Pen Tray

Besides the small rectangular tray, Plate 7 includes the pattern for a gold leaf pen tray. This provides more advanced practice in laying gold leaf. Proceed by the following stages:

1. Prepare the tray with three or four coats of flat black in the usual way. See Chapter 3.

2. Apply a thin film of whiting to prevent sticking as described earlier in this chapter.

3. Make a tracing of the pattern from Plate 7, and transfer it to the tray.

4. With a mixture of Yellow Ochre and varnish, and disregarding all superimposed details, paint the parts of the design which are to be gold in the following order, namely: the larger fruits, the smaller fruits, the leaves from the largest down to the smallest. This order ensures that, as far as possible, all will reach the proper tacky stage at the same time. Omit the tiny flowers, the buds, the stems, and the "whiskers," none of which are to be in gold. Then paint the end pieces, which are entirely in gold. When the proper tacky stage has been reached, lay the gold leaf. Wait one week.

5. Dust off the tray, and apply a coat of varnish to protect the gold. Let the work dry for 24 hours.

6. Rub very gently with the steel wool #000 to remove the gloss. Dust off thoroughly.

7. With a crow-quill pen and black ink, put in the lines and dots on the fruits and large leaves. Wait half an hour for the ink to harden.

8. Using a showcard brush, mix a little Burnt Sienna with varnish to make a transparent brown, and paint the shaded areas on the fruits, each time blending the edges at once with a clear varnish brush. Paint the tiny flowers and buds in off-white. Paint the stems and "whiskers" in mustard yellow. Let the work dry for 24 hours.

9. With Vermilion, paint the dots on the buds, and the circles on the flowers. The center dots on the flowers are done in black. Wait 24 hours.

10. With mustard yellow, paint a stripe around the edge of the tray.

11. Finish the tray in the usual way. (See Chapter 15.)

The central design of the pattern here dealt with can be seen in Photo. XIII (between pp. 38-39) of another type of pen tray.

XII GOLD LEAF BOX—5¼" × 8¼"

XIII GOLD LEAF PEN TRAY—9" long

XIV   RECTANGULAR GOLD LEAF TRAY

XV SMALL RECTANGULAR TRAY—9″ × 14″

XVI   LACE EDGE TRAY

XVII CHIPPENDALE TRAY

XVIII "QUEEN ANNE" TRAY—15" × 18"

XXX. SMALL OVAL GOLD LEAF TRAY. 10″ × 12″

II To Transfer a Design

Before a freehand design is painted on a tray, chair, or other object, an outline of the design should be transferred to the painted surface. The first step is to make a careful tracing of the design on tracing paper, including everything except the superimposed details, which can be added later by eye. Use a well-sharpened H or 2H pencil.

To Transfer to a Dark Background

1. Rub a cake of magnesium carbonate on the back of the tracing. Then, with your fingertips, rub this well into the paper. Blow off the excess powder.

2. Place the tracing, white side down, in position on the surface to be decorated, making sure the design is exactly where you want it. Then retrace the design with a well-sharpened 4H pencil.

It is not generally recommended that a tracing be taped down with masking tape while the design is being transferred. If this course is followed, however, use no more than two very small bits of tape, and be careful to wipe away any stickiness with Carbona Cleaning Fluid when the tape is removed. Taping down is, of course, not practicable on an uneven surface, such as a Chippendale tray border, where a tracing unavoidably shifts as you work. In this case, one can trace only an inch or two, after which the tracing must be readjusted.

To Transfer to a Light Background

1. On the back of the tracing, go over the pencil lines with a blunt H pencil. Do not use a soft pencil as it will smudge and spoil a light background.

2. Place the tracing right side up in the desired position on the painted surface, and retrace the design with a 4H pencil.

Home-made "Carbons"

Much of the time involved in the above-described process can be saved by using home-made "carbons." They can be used over and over again. (Commercial carbon papers generally are not suitable.)

A white "carbon" is made conveniently with a sheet of tracing paper about 6 by 12 inches. Rub the magnesium carbonate on one side of it, rubbing it well into the paper, and then blowing off the excess. With this sheet the necessity of putting magnesium carbonate on the backs of design tracings is done away with. You merely hold the tracing in position on the painted surface, and slip the "carbon," white side down, under the tracing. Holding both tracing and "carbon" in place with one hand, retrace the design, moving the "carbon" along when necessary. When not in use, fold the "carbon" in half, with the white inside.

A pencil "carbon," for use on light backgrounds, can be made in a similar way. Rub a piece of tracing paper all over one side with an H or 2H pencil.

12   To Enlarge or Reduce a Design

The method of enlarging a design will be explained step by step, taking the leaf shown in Plate 8 as the example.

1. Trace the leaf in the upper left-hand corner on a sheet of tracing paper large enough to contain also the enlarged size you want.

2. Draw a rectangle around the leaf that just boxes it in and touches it on all four sides. Use a small right-angled triangle or a postcard to get right angles at all the corners: Draw with a well-sharpened 2H pencil.

3. Extend the right-hand side of the rectangle downwards several inches, and extend the bottom line several inches out to the right.

4. Using a ruler, draw a line diagonally from the upper left-hand corner to the lower right one and beyond, as in the illustration.

5. Measure either the width or the height of the larger size that you want, and complete the larger rectangle. Use the triangle or the postcard to get right angles at the corners, and be sure the diagonal already drawn passes through the lower right-hand corner. This insures that the enlarged size will be in the same proportion as the original.

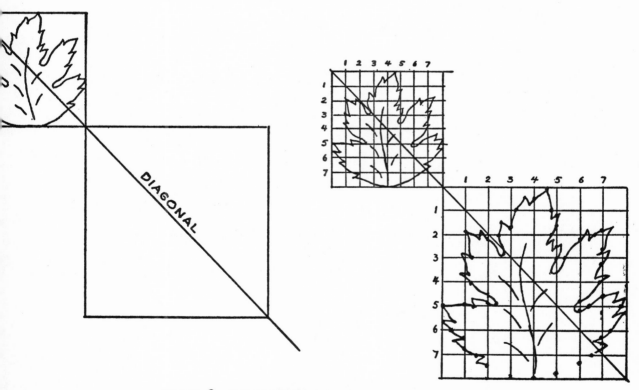

PLATE 8   ENLARGEMENT OF A DESIGN UNIT

6. With the ruler, divide the sides of the smaller rectangle in half, then in quarters, and then in eighths. Do the same with the larger rectangle. If the design is more complicated than our present example, divide the sides into sixteenths or even thirty-seconds.

7. Rule in the lines and number them, as shown in the illustration.

8. You will observe that the outline of the smaller leaf is crossed by the dividing lines at certain points in the little square. Where these points occur place a dot in the corresponding place on the larger square. Watch the numbers to be sure you are in the corresponding square each time. When all the dots are in, join them up with lines of the same character as those in the original.

9. If the finished leaf looks a little stiff, put a fresh piece of tracing paper over it, and retrace it. While doing this you have an opportunity to improve the drawing.

To *reduce* a design, turn Plate 8 upside down, and go through the same procedure, but this time you will be starting with the larger unit and ending up with the smaller size.

13   To Adapt a Design

Sometimes it happens that we want to use a particular pattern on a surface whose proportions do not correspond to it. The surface may be a little longer or a little shorter in one direction or another than was the case with the original from which the pattern was taken.

For example, the Gold Leaf Box Pattern in Plate 38 is 6 by 8¾ inches, and it was desired to use it on a box which was 5¼ by 8⅛ inches (see Photo. XII between pp. 38-39). Since the proportions were roughly the same, the pattern might have been reduced to fit the box. However, it was preferred to use the leaves and acorns in their original size. This was achieved by following these directions:

1. On a sheet of tracing paper, rule off an area the exact size of the surface you want to decorate. Rule a second line around the edge to complete the width of the stripe.

2. Mark the center of each side of the original pattern and of each side of the new size.

3. Since the main motifs of this pattern are at the centers of each side, put the center of one long side of the new size over the corresponding center of the pattern, and trace the main motif, which is the cluster of leaves and acorns. Do the same with each of the other three sides.

4. Then place the corresponding corners of the new size over the pattern, and trace the corner motifs.

5. Since there will not be room for the whole design, it will be necessary to leave out some of the tiny sprays, or an acorn; or to reduce the size of a leaf here and there. The important things to remember are to keep the main motifs intact, and to make the necessary changes where they will neither be noticed nor affect the balance of the design as a whole.

Conversely, should our pattern be somewhat smaller than the available working surface, we should have to add an acorn, a leaf, or a tiny spray somewhere between the main center motifs and the secondary corner motifs.

It is not advisable to adapt patterns to sizes that are a great deal larger or smaller than the original, as the composition or balance is almost sure to suffer as a result.

14   Striping

Striping is an important part of practically every decorating job. Examine almost any decorated article of the eighteenth or nineteenth century, and you will find that the design includes a painted fine-line stripe. Nothing will impart a "professional" touch to your work more than a well-executed bit of striping.

At first, this may seem difficult to achieve, but the fact is that striping is easily learned. It requires a certain amount of practice, but it is practice which steadies the hand, and you will soon gain a facility with the brush.

The proper brush for this work is a square-tipped camel's-hair, or badger hair, quill brush, with hairs about 1½ inches long, and about #1 in thickness. It is used without a handle, and in the act of striping, the brush is always pulled towards you. See Plate 19.

Begin by half-filling a bottle cap with varnish. Using a showcard brush, mix in with the varnish a little Japan Yellow and a touch of Burnt Umber, until the color is a fairly thin mustard yellow. With the brush, lift out some of the mixture on the newspaper palette. Dip the striper into the mixture on the palette, moderately loading it the full length of the hairs. Pull it back and forth on the newspaper to get the feel of the brush.

Practice striping first on a piece of back paper, always pulling the striper towards you. The stripe should be semi-transparent, about 1/16 inch or less in width, with the black paper partly showing through it to give it a slightly greenish cast. Some of the old trays have a hair-line opaque yellow stripe, which is obtained by adding to the mixture a little White or a little more Japan Yellow.

Students may find it helpful to practice striping on a raw tray, and thus get the feel of working on an object. The tin can easily be cleaned off with Carbona. With a striper adequately loaded with paint, you should be able to stripe one side of a tray without replenishing the brush.

In striping a chair slat with sharp corners, carry the stripe right to the edge of the slat each time. Then touch up the corners with the background paint when the stripe is dry.

These painted fine-line stripes, as distinct from the broader bronze stripes, are done on a glossy or varnished surface that is thoroughly dry. The glossy surface not only keeps the stripe from developing a fuzzy edge, but also permits corrections which, however, must be done at once, either with a clean cloth or by means of Carbona. If your hand seems to stick as you stripe, put a little talcum powder on the fingertips.

The broader bronze stripes are done on a flat painted surface and are painted in the same manner as a freehand gold pattern. The stripe is painted in a mixture of Japan Vermilion and varnish; when it is tacky, the gold powder is applied with velvet.

On a stenciled tray or chair it is easier to paint the bronze stripes before you do the stenciling, as you still have the flat paint surface on which to work. When the stripes are thoroughly dry, and all loose powder has been carefully removed with a damp sponge, the surface may be varnished for stenciling.

Some beginners like to cut a stencil for the broad gold stripes and stencil them on in the usual way, but there are many jobs where this course is not practicable. Moreover, a stenciled stripe is apt to have a rigid, stilted look. There is nothing to equal a well-executed hand-painted stripe, and with practice you will be able to do it.

15 Antiquing and Finishing

To achieve the effect of the finish found on most old pieces, we apply at least six coats of varnish after the decoration has been completed. On trays and table tops, for which a heat-proof and alcohol-resistant surface is always desirable, the last two coats should be of Super Valspar varnish, procurable in most paint stores.

Some of the coats of varnish may be toned with oil pigments to give an antique color, and this process we call antiquing. The varnish so tinted must remain completely transparent, and therefore only a very little color should be used to make it. Otherwise unsightly streaks will appear on the decorated surface. For most purposes we use Burnt Umber or Raw Umber, but Indian Yellow, Black, or Prussian Blue are occasionally used. Antiquing is generally done with the first coat, or the first two or three coats, depending on the depth of color you want. Since most beginners tend to over-antique, it is well to act on the principle that a little antiquing goes a long way.

It is important to do all varnishing in an atmosphere free from dust. Clean the room first, and allow the dust to settle. Close the windows, and while the varnish is drying keep traffic away from the room for the first three or four hours.

Varnish should be applied in a warm room, one in which the temperature is 70 degrees or more. The varnish itself should be at least that warm, and so should the object to be varnished. To achieve this, let each stand in the room for some time before the varnishing is begun. They may be placed near a radiator to raise their temperature a little. Varnish applied to a cold surface, or in a cold room will "crawl."

Taking a tin tray as our example, we will now go step by step through the procedure of finishing and antiquing it.

First Day

Dust the tray carefully and place it on clean newspapers. Decide where to put the tray to dry after it has been varnished, and spread newspapers there with a can or other firm object in the middle on which the wet tray may finally be rested. Just before beginning to varnish, wipe the tray with the palm of your hand to remove any remaining lint or dust particles, especially from the corners.

On a clean newspaper palette squeeze out a little Burnt Umber. Using your one-inch varnish brush, dip out four or five brushfuls of varnish,

46

and mix with them on the palette a touch of Burnt Umber. Try it out on a clean piece of paper to test the color, which should not be much darker than the clear varnish itself. Work quickly because varnish thickens on contact with the air.

If it is the right color, that is, a very pale brown, start to varnish the tray at once, first doing the underside of the flange, then the edge, then the top side of the flange, and finally the floor. Don't flood the varnish on, as it will only run down and settle in the corners, where it cannot dry properly. Spread it out, and work with the light falling across your work so as to enable you to see that every bit of surface is covered. Then use the brush in the crosswise direction to ensure an even distribution.

Work quickly, and mix more varnish and Burnt Umber as you need it. In doing so, keep a sharp watch lest any brown streaks appear, for that would mean that you have added too much color to the varnish. Last of all, hold the tray high, and pick up with the brush any varnish drippings from the under side. Set the tray down on the prepared stand, and leave it to dry for 24 hours.

Second Day

Dust off the tray, and apply the second coat of varnish, adding a touch of Burnt Umber if you want a darker color. Dry for 24 hours.

Third Day

Dust off, and then apply the third coat of varnish. Dry for 24 hours.

Fourth Day

Cut some very fine sandpaper into 1½ by 3½ inch pieces, and fold them in half, with the sand outside. Sandpaper the surface with these small pieces. Starting on the floor of the tray, sandpaper diagonally, first from upper left to lower right, and next from upper right to lower left. Work on small sections in turn. When one hand is tired, use the other, and by thus changing back and forth you will save time and not become fatigued.

Although sandpapering has to be thorough, you must be careful not to do it too long or to press too hard, for you may go right through the coats of varnish. Once the floor of the tray has been sanded, do the flanges, keeping away from the edges, where the sandpaper can very easily take off both varnish and paint. Naturally, this caution must be observed in dealing with any kind of object, large or small.

Sanding being completed, dust off the tray. If any sand particles are stuck in the corners, it means you used too much varnish previously, and that it was unable to dry properly. In such a case, you will have to wait another 24 hours for the varnish to dry, after which the corners may be sanded out.

Apply the fourth coat of varnish, and allow it to dry for 24 hours.

Fifth Day

Sandpaper the surface as described above. Dust off thoroughly. Apply a coat of Super Valspar varnish. This is a heavier varnish than the previous coats so that you must work quickly and vigorously to brush it all over the surface before it starts to set. Let it dry for 24 hours.

Sixth Day

Instead of sandpaper, use steel wool #000, rubbing on the diagonal again. In dusting off, be sure to get all the remnants of steel wool out of the corners. Apply the second coat of Super Valspar, and let it dry for 48 hours.

Final Rubbing

In the center of the tray place about a teaspoonful of powdered pumice. Take a soft cotton flannel cloth, and put a little crude oil on it. Dip the oiled cloth into the pumice, and begin to rub a small section of the tray, say, about five inches square, at a time. There is no need to rub long, for the high gloss of the varnish comes off immediately. If you rub too much, you will give the tray a dull, lifeless finish, whereas the proper effect is that of a satiny gleam. This is achieved very quickly and without strenuous effort. Use enough crude oil to keep the rubbing moist.

When you have gone over the whole tray, rub off the remains of the oil and pumice with a clean flannelette cloth, and let the surface dry. In about fifteen minutes inspect the surface, and if any bright glossy spots are visible, give them a rubbing as before. Wipe off again with a clean cloth. This satiny finish needs no furniture polish to preserve it. All it needs is the application now and then of a damp cloth.

16   Restoring Decorated Articles

The restoration of decorated antiques should be undertaken only after one has studied many original pieces and has acquired considerable skill in all the painting methods. Obviously a higher degree of practical experience and skill is required for the restoration of valuable antiques than for reproducing them. The following paragraphs give an outline of the procedures.

The first point to be considered is whether the decoration is genuinely old, and the second is whether it has sufficient merit to justify restoration. Experience is the best guide. Worth-while decorations are recognized by their sure and expert brushwork, their evidence of beautifully cut stencils, and their well-balanced designs.

Cleaning

A piece which is to be restored should be washed gently and judiciously with mild soap and water so as to remove surface dirt. Rinse and dry. For any white stains or thick coatings of old shellac, use denatured alcohol, but only a little at a time. Watch closely its effect on the decoration. If any color comes off on the cloth, stop at once. Work only on a small section at a time. A white film may be left, but this will disappear when a coat of varnish is applied.

If there is a coat of paint over an original decoration, it must be removed slowly and carefully. Sometimes a continued application of soap on a damp cloth will do. In other cases rubbing small sections at a time with denatured alcohol is effective. Or the coating may be removable by chipping it off bit by bit with a small knife. In all cases judgment and discretion must be exercised if the decoration below is to be preserved.

Rust

For removing rust spots, use the Deoxidine solution in the regular way. This will not harm paint, but in rubbing the spots with steel wool, rub the surrounding paint or decoration as little as possible. Rinse and dry. Then apply a coat of varnish as a protection against further rust. Dry 24 hours.

Partial Restoration

Whenever possible, keep the original decoration, touching in only where the decoration and background are missing. Match the colors as closely as you can. Bronze powders may be mixed on the newspaper palette with a little varnish and oil color. Let the touched-up parts dry for 24 hours, and then "antique" them with transparent overtones, to match the original.

Complete Restoration

When a decoration is too far gone to be restored, make a careful and complete copy of it on frosted acetate. This is done by first making an accurate tracing on frosted acetate of everything that is even faintly visible. Sometimes all one can see of the original gold scrolls are faint impressions on the black paint. Next, put a fresh piece of frosted acetate over this tracing, and make a complete painted copy. Supply any missing sections from research or imagination.

Having thus prepared your pattern, you can proceed to remove the old finish entirely from the article and start the work of restoration on the raw metal.

Pitted Areas

Sometimes the floor of an old tray is badly pitted where the paint has been chipped off. To deal with such areas, take some thick sediment from the bottom of a can of flat black, and mix it with enough powdered pumice to make a heavy paste. Add a few drops of varnish. Use this compound as a filler, smoothing it on with a small palette knife or your finger. Let this dry several days, and then sandpaper it. For a colored background, use the appropriate color instead of flat black.

Restoration of a Stenciled Design

To restore a stenciled design, proceed as follows:

1. Trace the design carefully on frosted acetate.

2. Placing the architect's tracing linen over the acetate, trace the outlines of the missing sections. Cut stencils for these.

3. Varnish the tray or other surface, and, when it is tacky, stencil the missing parts, matching the bronze powders as closely as possible. Let the work dry for 24 hours.

4. Using varnish toned with a little oil color, apply a transparent overtone to "antique" the newly stenciled parts, and to make them match the original parts as far as possible. Use as little varnish as you can, so that it will not form a ridge around the edges when it settles. When desirable, flatten or smooth out the edges of the varnish patch with the tip of your finger.

Another method is to give the whole tray a coat of varnish; then, immediately wiping most of the varnish off the brush, pick up the smallest bit of dry color on the brush, and lightly go over the newer parts until you obtain the color you want. Sometimes it is necessary to use a smaller brush in applying the color. The process requires considerable skill to put the color just where you want it and to avoid streakiness.

5. Finish the article in the usual way with several coats of varnish.

Golf Leaf Restoration

To match gold leaf truly is very difficult, if not impossible. However, since restoration is better than neglect, we should try to do the best we can. Make a tracing of the original pattern, and supply the missing parts. Transpose these to the prepared surface. Then apply the gold leaf in the usual way over a mixture of varnish and Yellow Ochre. Let the gold leaf dry for a week, after which apply a protective coat of varnish. When this is dry, use transparent-colored overtones over the newly laid gold leaf to match as closely as possible the color of the old metal.

Restoration of Old Painted Chests and Boxes

These usually have an oil finish, that is, the designs were painted with colors mixed with turpentine and linseed oil. This sort of finish requires an oiling once a year to keep it in good condition. First, clean the surface by washing it carefully and gently. Wait 24 hours, and then oil the surface with raw linseed oil, applied on a soft cloth. Give the oil at least a week to soak in, and meanwhile keep the dust from settling on it.

If any parts of the design need restoring, this should be done with Japan and oil colors, mixed with Turpentine, linseed oil, and a few drops of Japan Dryer to hasten the drying. Any colors containing linseed oil require at least a week to dry thoroughly. It is important to remember this when imposing one color on another.

17 Adapting Used Furniture

Not everyone possesses decorated antiques, but it is nearly true to say that everyone possesses used pieces of ordinary furniture which, instead of being discarded, could be transformed by painting and decorating into admired and still useful adjuncts to the home. For example, a chest of drawers, if the drawers work smoothly, and the piece is of good proportions, should never be abandoned. Make it instead an object lesson in the value of American antique decoration.

A chair pattern often makes a good decoration for a chest of drawers. The main design is used on the top drawer and the accessory units, such as those in Plates 27 and 40, being added to suit the construction of the piece. Tiny borders, applied around the edge of each drawer, are sometimes most effective, and may be all that is needed. Any striping should be in mustard yellow if applied to our usual black background color. The freehand bronze chair pattern in Plate 16 might be used for a chest of drawers having a pale yellow or off-white background, in conjunction with brown and black striping.

For a cabinet with two small doors, the watering can pattern would be good. Coffee tables, end tables, and bookcases might be decorated effectively with some of the borders in Plate 26. In this kind of work there is an opportunity to use judgment and decorate according to the shape and size of the furniture. Of course, we must always resist the temptation to over-decorate.

Country patterns are very suitable for kitchen furniture and fittings and likewise for porch and outdoor furniture.

Gold leaf decorations make for elegance, invariably attracting more attention than the other techniques. For this very reason particularly careful attention should be given to their application. As a suggestion, the large oval tray pattern in Plate 37 would look very fine around the edge of a simple but really well-designed coffee table. Such a splendid pattern, however, would be quite out of place on many pieces. Suit the pattern to the character of the object.

Additional Patterns

The instructions which accompany the following drawings are kept as short as is consistent with clarity. Needless repetition is avoided. It is a simple matter to refer back to the chapters on background painting, on gold leaf, and on the other fundamental processes whenever they are mentioned and it is found that the memory needs to be refreshed.

18 Pennsylvania Chest

This pattern is taken from a pine chest made in Berks County, Pennsylvania, and dated on the front, 1798. The chest measures 48 inches long, 23 inches high, and 21 inches deep. Study the drawing on the title page of this book in order to determine how much to enlarge the pattern for your own purpose. The proportions of the chest to which the pattern is to be adapted will be your guide.

To prepare an old chest for decoration, remove the existing paint and varnish, and apply a coat of shellac. When this is dry, sandpaper the surface.

Before any painting is done, the outline of the pilasters and the arches (not the floral design) should be transferred to the front of the chest. Place the chest on its back so that you can do the work comfortably.

The background of the two panels formed by the pilasters and arches should now be painted in a dull ivory, made by mixing White, Yellow Ochre, and a touch of Raw Umber.

The background of the rest of the chest is in a light brown, made by adding a little White to Burnt Sienna. Mix it in a small jar with a showcard brush. Use tube oil colors, and add very little varnish, thus keeping the mixture quite thick. As you use it, lift out small quantities at a time on to the newspaper palette. Apply the color to the chest with a damp sponge, a little at a time and not too much in any one place. Allow the natural wood to show through and give to the whole surface the effect of a texture. Wait 24 hours.

Referring to the title page sketch, paint the black parts of the pilasters and arches, and the black parts of the corners, in a brown similar to that used for the background, but this time use a darker shade. This will be achieved by using a little less of the White with the Burnt Sienna. Let the work dry for 24 hours. Paint the remaining parts of the pilasters in Japan Vermilion. Allow 24 hours for drying.

For the designs on the ivory panels, turn to Plate 9. With Japan Black, paint all the parts there shown in black. Use this color also for the initials and the date between the panels in the event that you wish to include them. Wait 24 hours.

All the dotted areas are to be painted in Japan Vermilion, and this should be thinned with varnish so that when the color is applied over the

DULL IVORY
BACKGROUND

BS

BS

BS

BS

BS

BS

BS

BS

BS

BS

BS

BS

PLATE 9   PENNSYLVANIA CHEST

black "speckles" in the center of the main flower, in the lower tulips, and elsewhere, the speckles will show through the red, and appear brownish. Wait 24 hours.

Mix Japan Yellow and a little Burnt Sienna to make a rich, warm, mustard yellow, adding enough varnish to make this also slightly thin. With this mixture, paint all those parts which are diagonally shaded. Paint right over the black markings in the upper tulips. These markings will show grayish through the slightly transparent yellow. With a thicker mixture of the same yellow, paint the outlines around the hearts at the corners of the chest.

The parts marked BS are painted with the same light brown which was used for the sponged background process, and this also should be slightly thin so that the black spreckles on the vase show through a little.

Old Pennsylvania chests were not painted with varnish or given finishing coats of varnish. If an old chest is being restored and needs no more than a little touching up here and there, it is desirable to mix your colors with turpentine and linseed oil, as was done by the old decorators. But to keep paint of that kind in good condition it is necessary to rub it over with raw linseed oil once a year. Therefore, if you are starting from the very beginning on an old chest, you will probably prefer to use varnish in mixing the colors and to finish up with the six coats of varnish generally recommended. That kind of finish not only wears better, but once it is applied it needs little or no attention.

19 Coffee Pot

PLATE 10—ILLUSTRATION FACING P. xii

The original coffee pot illustrated was painted with a background of asphaltum, but the pattern is just as effective on a black background, which besides is much easier to apply. A practice copy of this pattern being desirable, put a piece of frosted acetate over Plate 10. The large circular area behind the design is in off-white, but this may be omitted on the acetate copy.

1. With Japan Vermilion, paint the large over-all areas marked V, without regard to the dotted and shaded areas, and the other details on them. To avoid misunderstanding, refer to the small drawing in the left-hand bottom corner of Plate 10, where it is made plain that the entire areas marked V are to be painted Vermilion, leaving the colors indicated by the dotting, shading, etc., to be superimposed later, as described lower down.

With a country green mixture, paint all the solid black areas, representing the leaves.

With a soft medium blue, paint the two flowers and the fruit marked B, again ignoring details and shaded areas.

Similarly disregarding the presence of the cross-hatched area and the details, paint the single fruit at the bottom, marked Y, with a light mustard yellow. Wait 24 hours.

2. Mix Alizarin Crimson and a touch of Burnt Umber with enough varnish to make a rich, dark, semi-transparent red, and paint all the finely dotted areas.

With Japan Vermilion, apply a broad stroke or two on the cross-hatched area of the yellow fruit at the bottom, blending off the inner edge with a clear varnish brush. Wait 24 hours.

3. With a thin, semi-transparent, mustard yellow, paint the shaded areas on the three vermilion flowers and on the upper half of the large center stem. Do likewise with the shaded areas on the blue flower at the lower left, and on the blue flower at the upper left, in the latter case blending off the edge all around. Apply the yellow also to the blue fruit, blending off the inner edge, and to the small shaded leaf at the extreme left of the drawing. Wait 24 hours.

4. With Japan Black, paint all the leaf veins, the tiny clusters of dots,

58

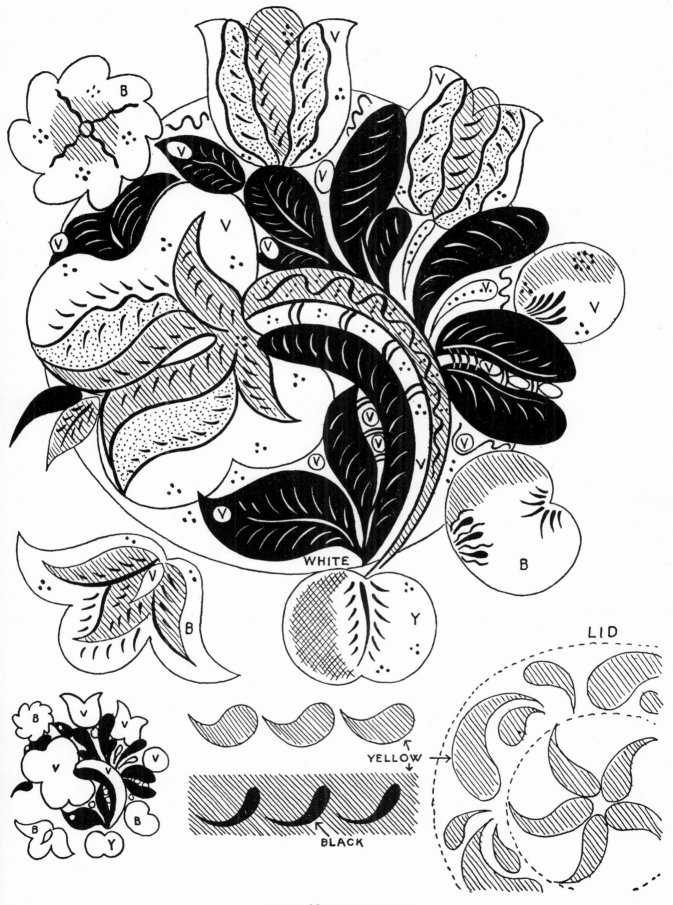

WHITE

LID

YELLOW →

BLACK

PLATE 10   COFFEE POT

the heavy black outlines, and all the other details shown in black in the drawing. Similarly outline the green leaves.

To decorate the coffee pot, prepare the background with three or four coats of the usual flat black, or, if desired, with asphaltum (see page 15).

1. Make a tracing of the design, including the large circular area. This has a diameter of 5¼ inches and should be drawn with a compass. Transfer the circle first to the coffee pot. Remove the tracing, and paint the circular area in off-white. Wait 24 hours.

2. Transfer the rest of the design to the coffee pot.

3. Proceed to paint the pattern as described above. The brush-stroke border and the strokes on the lid are in mustard yellow. Let dry 24 hours.

5. Paint the hairline striping in mustard yellow, according to the construction of the coffee pot.

6. Finish the piece in the usual way.

20 Sugar Bowl

PLATE 11—ILLUSTRATION FACING P. xii

The original background was asphaltum, but unless you have had a good deal of practice in applying asphaltum, it is advisable to prepare the sugar bowl with a flat black background in the usual way.

1. Take a sheet of tracing paper long enough to go entirely around the bowl. Hold it against the bowl, and trace the line of the top edge, marking where the ends meet. This will give you a curved line for the upper edge of the border. Using a ruler, mark off a number of points below the line at a distance equal to the width of the border. Join the points by a second curved line, parallel to the first. You now have a border area which will go exactly around your bowl. If you are putting the design on a canister instead of a bowl, the border is more easily made, since the parallel lines will be straight.

In either case, the next step is to trace the motifs from Plate 11, rearranging them a little if necessary to ensure a continuous sequence without any noticeable join. Trace also the brush-stroke border. Make a separate tracing for the lid pattern.

2. Transfer the border area to the bowl or canister. Transfer the four circular areas on the lid. Paint both border and circular areas throughout in off-white. Wait 24 hours.

3. Transfer the rest of the design to the bowl.

4. With Japan Vermilion, paint the whole area of the fruits marked V, covering the details and the shading up to the curved right-hand edge of the fruit. Paint the strokes marked V on the lid.

With a country green mixture, paint the large leaves which are black in the drawing.

With a soft medium blue, paint the strokes marked B on the lid. Wait 24 hours.

5. With a semi-transparent mustard yellow, paint the shaded areas on the border, blending off the inner edge. Paint the brush-stroke border and the shaded brush strokes on the lid. Wait 24 hours.

6. With Japan Black, paint all the veins, clusters of dots, and the details on the fruit.

7. Striping at the top and bottom edges of the bowl and around the edge of the lid is in mustard yellow.

8. Finish in the usual way.

WHITE BORDER

LID

B V B V B V B V B

VERMILION
GREEN
YELLOW

PLATE 11 (UPPER) SUGAR BOWL; (LOWER) COFFEE POT

21 *Coffee Pot Pattern Applied to Box*

PLATE 11—ILLUSTRATION FACING P. xii

This design was taken from an old coffee pot and in the illustration is shown applied to a round flat box. It can, of course, be applied to other suitably shaped objects. The original background was black. To paint the design, proceed as follows:

1. With Japen Vermilion, paint all the petals marked V, including their shaded and dotted areas.

With a country green mixture, paint the areas which are black in the illustration. Allow 24 hours to dry.

2. Mix Alizarin Crimson and a touch of Burnt Umber to make a transparent dark red, and paint the dotted brush strokes.

With a semi-transparent mixture of off-white, paint the shaded brush strokes. Wait 24 hours.

3. Paint the remaining brush strokes a mustard yellow. In the drawing these are the white areas, apart from those marked V.

4. Striping is in mustard yellow.

22 Coffin Tray

PLATE 12—ILLUSTRATION FACING P. xii

Coffin trays, or country octagonal trays, were made in this country by the local tinsmith and were generally decorated with the gaily colored designs we have come to know as country painting. Gold leaf was more or less unknown to the country tinsmith, although, from about 1820, many of his wares were stenciled with bronze powders.

Plate 12 shows the pattern for the coffin tray. To carry out the work, proceed as follows:

1. Paint the tray flat black in the usual way.

2. Make a tracing of the design from Plate 12, and transfer it to the tray.

3. Mix some Japan Vermilion, Yellow Ochre, and White to make a salmon pink, and with this mixture, paint the flowers and the buds (marked S) and likewise the stems. Cover the shaded and dotted areas as well as the white parts of the flowers and buds.

With a mixture of country green, paint all those leaves (G) which are black in Plate 12. Wait 24 hours.

4. Mix Alizarin Crimson and a touch of Burnt Umber to make a semi-transparent dark red, and apply this to the dotted areas on the flowers and buds, using only one stroke each time.

With a semi-transparent mustard yellow, paint the highlights on the leaves as indicated by the dotted white lines.

With a somewhat thicker mixture of mustard yellow, paint all the white leaves (Y); the cross-hatching at the center of the flower on the right; and the border strokes. Wait 24 hours.

5. With a semi-transparent off-white, paint the shaded strokes on the flowers and buds. Wait 24 hours.

6. Give the tray a coat of varnish to provide a glossy surface for striping. Wait 24 hours.

7. Add the striping in mustard yellow.

8. Finish the tray in the usual way.

PLATE 12 COFFIN TRAY

23   Deed Box

PLATE 13—ILLUSTRATION FACING P. xii

The fruit border is painted on a band of off-white that goes around the sides of the black painted box.

Refer to Plate 13. With Japan Vermilion, paint the over-all areas of the fruits and berries marked V.

With a light country green mixture, paint the leaves marked LG. Wait 24 hours.

With a light mustard yellow, paint the shaded areas on the vermilion fruits and berries, blending off the edges with varnish. Wait 24 hours.

Using Japan Black, paint the brush-strokes on the fruits, the tiny clusters of dots, and the leaf veins.

The brush-stroke designs and border on the cover of the box, and the striping are all done in light mustard yellow.

BLACK

WHITE

LG

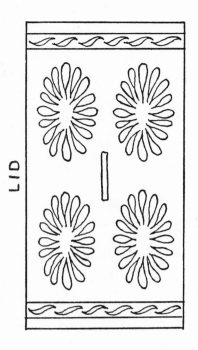

LID

BLACK

WHITE

LG

PLATE 13 DEED BOX

24 Cedar Wood Box Pattern: Lamp

PLATE 14—ILLUSTRATION P. xii

1. Refer to Plate 14. With Japan Vermilion, paint the outer section of the tulip and the buds (V), covering the details and the dotted areas.

With a country green mixture, paint the leaves and stems, shown in solid black in the drawing.

With a yellow green mixture, paint the scrolls at the top (LG). Wait 24 hours.

2. With a mixture of Alizarin Crimson and Burnt Umber, paint the dotted strokes on the vermilion flowers and buds.

Using a light mustard yellow, paint the horizontally shaded areas of the tulip. Fill the space between with a cross-hatching of yellow lines as in the drawing. The dots at the points of the buds are also to be done in yellow (Y).

With a light blue mixture, paint the small bands on the buds (LB).

Paint the leaf veins in Burnt Umber.

25 Tea Caddy

PLATE 14—ILLUSTRATION P. xii

1. Using off-white, paint the overall areas of the flower and the detached "buds." See Plate 14. Cover the dotted areas as well as those which are blank in the drawing.

With a light country green mixture, paint the leaves and stems shown black in the drawing. Wait 24 hours.

2. Paint the dotted areas on the flower and on the "buds" with a mixture of Alizarin Crimson and Burnt Umber.

Paint the ring of dots and the circular center of the flower with Burnt Sienna. These are cross-hatched in the drawing.

Paint the remaining leaves and stems (diagonally shaded) and the scrolls or tendrils in a light mustard yellow.

PLATE 14 (UPPER) CEDAR WOOD BOX; (LOWER) TEA CADDY

26 Small Rectangular Tray

PLATE 15—PHOTO. XV (BETWEEN PP. 38-39)

To make a practice copy of the floor design, place a sheet of frosted acetate over Plate 15, and proceed as follows:

1. With a mixture of medium blue, paint the flower and the two buds.

With a bright country green mixture, paint the leaves, stems, and the calyx on each bud. Wait 24 hours.

2. Mix some Prussian Blue and Raw Umber to make a transparent blue, and, referring to the photograph, apply this to darken one side of each flower petal and bud, blending off into the lighter half with varnish. Apply the same mixture to make the darker side of each leaf and calyx. Let the work dry for 24 hours.

3. To a thin mixture of off-white add a touch of Prussian Blue and Indian Yellow to give it a slightly greenish tinge, and, keeping the brush rather dry, apply this to the lighter side of each petal and bud, blending off the internal edge with varnish. Immediately pick up some dry White to add a white highlight to the wet surface. Do the complete operation on one petal at a time.

Using a bright mustard yellow, apply this to the lighter side of each leaf and each calyx. Blend off the inner edge, and on some of the leaves add a touch of *dry* yellow to the wet surface as a highlight. Wait 24 hours.

4. Paint a small dab of Vermilion on the center of the flower. Wait 24 hours.

5. Paint the stamens a mustard yellow, and add a touch of it on the vermilion.

BLACK BACKGROUND

GOLD LEAF BORDER

PLATE 15   SMALL RECTANGULAR TRAY—9″ × 12″

27 Chair Pattern in Freehand Bronze

PLATE 16—PHOTO. X (BETWEEN PP. 22-23)

The background color on the original chair was a soft, pale, antique yellow, made by taking flat white paint and adding Japan Yellow and a little Raw Umber. The pattern is done in palegold powder on a black underpainting.

To make a copy of the pattern, proceed as follows:

1. From Plate 16 trace the outline of the main design on tracing paper. Mount the tracing on white cardboard so that the lines can be seen easily, and put a piece of frosted acetate over it.

2. Trace, cut, and number the stencil units 1, 2, 3, 4, and 5.

3. With a mixture of Japan Black and varnish, paint the design, doing first the large main area, then the grapes, the separate brush strokes, and the tendrils. Let it dry until it has reached the proper tacky stage for stenciling.

4. Referring to the photograph for guidance, place the pear stencil (1) in position, and apply the palegold powder, making the highlights very bright. Leave the parts around the edges dark. Lift the stencil.

5. Place the leaf tip stencils (4 and 5) in position, and apply powder, making the highlights very bright, as shown in the photograph.

6. Next, stencil the cherries and plums (2 and 3).

7. Without using a stencil, apply the gold highlights on the large leaves, small leaves, grapes, lower end of pear, small leaf strokes, and tendrils. Let the work dry 24 hours.

8. Using a mixture of Japan Black and varnish, paint the outlines of the fruit, the fruit details, highlights on the grapes, leaf veins, the lower edges of the brush-strokes, and any other black accents needed. Wait 24 hours.

The striping on the chair consists of two bands of black, one broader than the other, and of a band of transparent umber, as shown in the middle of Plate 16.

STRIPING {

STENCILS

PLATE 16 CHAIR PATTERN IN FREEHAND BRONZE

28   Stenciled Hitchcock-Type Chair

PLATES 17 AND 19—PHOTO. III (BETWEEN PP. 22-23)

1. Prepare a Hitchcock-type chair with three or four coats of flat black.

2. Refer to Plate 19. The broad black stripes on the side back posts and on the small back slat are to be done in palegold, as are also the turnings marked in black on the front legs and the front rung, on the seat front, and on the chair back. Paint all these parts with a mixture of varnish and Japan Vermilion, and when the surface is tacky, apply the palegold powder with a velvet finger. Let the work dry for 24 hours. Then wipe off the loose powder with a damp sponge.

3. Trace and cut the stencil units shown in Plate 17, making separate stencils for the veins of the leaves. Number the units in ink to correspond with the numbers in Plate 17, and also write on each the name of the colored powder or powders to be used with it. Of course, the stenciling of this pattern should be practiced several times on black paper before the decoration of an actual chair is undertaken.

4. Varnish the main slat of the chair, the two side back posts, the seat front, and the hand grip.

5. When the varnished surface of the main slat is ready for stenciling, turn to the photograph of the pattern (Photo. III), and proceed to stencil in accordance with it. The best position for the chair during stenciling is to have it lying on its back on the work table. To take full advantage of this position you should stencil upside down, with the pattern from which you are copying also turned upside down.

Stencil border unit (1) in palegold on each side of the slat.

Place the bowl (3) in position, and the leaf (2) in position on top of it. Holding the leaf in place, remove the bowl. Stencil the leaf in palegold, very bright around the edge, shading quickly to black in the center. Lift the stencil and put the bowl back in place, stenciling it in palegold, very bright at the center, shading off slightly at the side, and leaving some black all around the leaf (2).

Place (4) in position in the center, and stencil first the brightest part at the top in palegold; then shade in a little fire powder, but quickly let it go to black. Place (5) in position, and complete the peach. Stencil the second peach.

Proceed in numerical order with the rest of the units in the main

76

11 FIRE

3 PALEGOLD

2

7
PALEGOLD
& FIRE

8

9 SILVER

6
PALEGOLD
& FIRE

10
PALEGOLD

1

4   5
PALEGOLD
& FIRE

16   15

DEEPGOLD

14

13
SILVER

12
PALEGOLD

17 HAND GRIP
PALEGOLD

18

SEAT FRONT IN PALEGOLD

PLATE 17   STENCILED HITCHCOCK-TYPE CHAIR

slat, always referring to the photograph for the light and dark areas. The veins are all in deep gold.

Plate 19 shows where the accessory units are placed on the side back posts, the handgrip, and the seat front. All are in palegold. Let the work dry for 24 hours. Then wipe off any loose powder with a damp sponge.

6. Apply a coat of varnish to the entire chair to provide a glossy surface for the striping. Allow 24 hours to dry.

7. The hair-line striping is done in mustard yellow, and its placing more or less depends on the construction of the chair. In the example in Plate 19, there is a fine stripe around the edge of each slat, one to outline the flattened areas on the side back posts, others around the edge of the sides of the seat, on the seat front, and on some of the turnings, as shown by the fine pen lines.

8. Finish the chair in the usual way.

29 Stenciled Village Scene

PLATES 18 AND 19—PHOTO. II (BETWEEN PP. 22-23)

Stenciled scenes like this one were great favorites in the old days and were used on chairs, trays, boxes, cornices, and other pieces. The original stencils for this scene (preserved in the Metropolitan Museum of Art, New York) are two in number; but it is more helpful in adapting the design to have separate stencils for each feature, as shown in the Plates. To make a copy on black paper, proceed as follows:

1. Trace and cut the stencil units shown in Plates 18 and 19. Unit (1) consists of the courthouse and two trees; (1A), a separate unit, is part of the courthouse, but stenciled separately. (2) and (2A) likewise form a pair, as do (3) and (3A). Number the stencil pieces to correspond with the drawings.

2. Varnish a sheet of black paper, size 15 by 6 inches.

3. When the proper tacky stage is reached, place stencil (1) in position, using the photograph as a guide, and stencil it in palegold. Next stencil group (2) in palegold, and then (3), also in palegold. (Note: information being lacking as to the colors of the powders originally used for this pattern, probable and appropriate ones are here supplied.)

Place (1A) in position over the already stenciled courthouse, and apply fire powder to the roof and faintly around the edges of the building so as to give it an air of substance. Do the same with the other buildings.

Stencil (4) in palegold and (4A) in silver. (5) and (6) follow, also in palegold.

Wait another 15 or 20 minutes to allow the surface to become a little drier and then, with very little palegold on the velvet, faintly cloud the ground. Then apply faint touches of silver to the sky.

PLATE 18   STENCILED VILLAGE SCENE—SECTION A

30 Stenciled Rectangular Tray

PLATE 20—PHOTO. V (BETWEEN PP. 22-23)

The tray here described is 15 by 20 inches in size. It should be painted flat black in the usual way. Then proceed as follows:

1. Cut a sheet of tracing paper the same size as the tray floor, rule a line ⅛ inch from the edge of the paper to indicate the gold band, and transfer the outline of the band to the tray. Study Plate 20 where the band is shown in its relation to the flange line. Paint the band with a mixture of varnish and Japan Vermilion, and, when the surface is tacky, apply palegold powder. Wait 24 hours.

2. Referring to Plate 20, trace the stencil units on linen in the usual way; with the exception of (2), which has the leaf vein extending out at one end of the linen, as illustrated. When this unit is all cut out, the linen may be folded so that the vein will lie in its correct position on the leaf.

3. Cut the stencils, and number the pieces as on Plate 20. (As with other new stenciling projects, a practice copy of the pattern on black paper is advisable before decorating the tray.)

4. Varnish the tray for stenciling. While waiting, study the photograph (Photo. V), and cut a piece of tracing linen, size 5⅝ by 3½ inches, with rounded corners. When the varnished surface is ready for stenciling, lay this linen in the exact center of the tray, checking with a ruler to be sure it is centered. Your floor border will lie between the linen and the gold band.

5. Begin to stencil by placing unit (1) in the exact center of one side, checking with a ruler. Stencil the flower in palegold, very bright around the outside, but shading slightly to darker in the center. Refer continually to the photograph. There is a flower on each side of the center one, and these are also in palegold at this stage. (Twenty-four hours later, when the stenciling is dry, these two flowers are given an overtone of transparent red.)

Stencil a group of three palegold flowers on each of the other three sides of the tray floor.

6. Place the cut-out leaf (2) in position, and then press down the vein in position on the leaf. Stencil the vein first with a silver-palegold mixture all around the very edge of the vein, stopping before you touch any part of the flowers already done. Mix the powder right on the velvet by

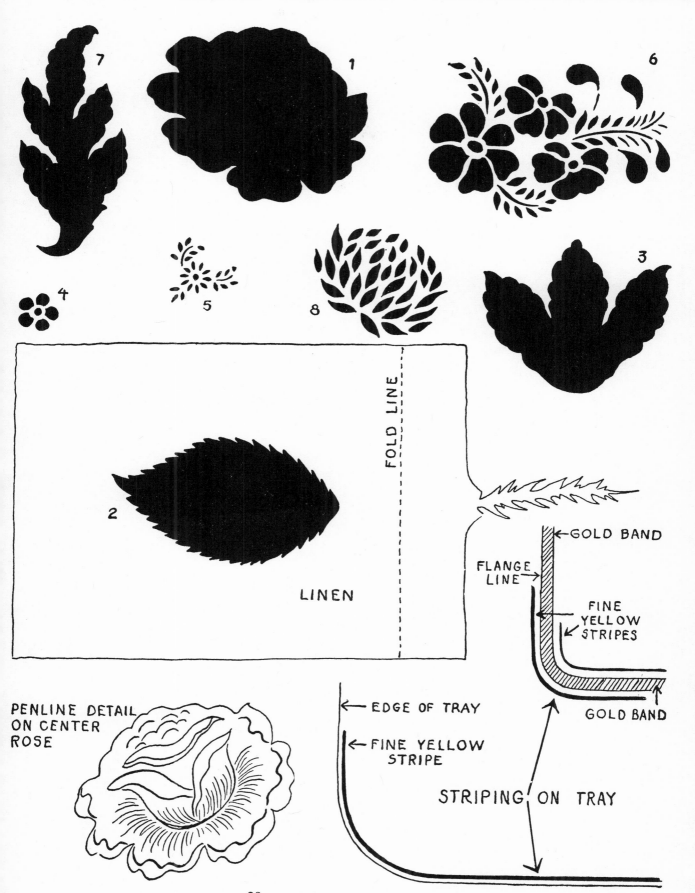

FOLD LINE

LINEN

GOLD BAND

FLANGE LINE

FINE YELLOW STRIPES

GOLD BAND

EDGE OF TRAY

FINE YELLOW STRIPE

STRIPING ON TRAY

PENLINE DETAIL ON CENTER ROSE

PLATE 20   STENCILED RECTANGULAR TRAY

taking up first a little silver and then a little gold. Next, apply the mixed powder around the outer edge of the leaf, leaving a darker area between. Repeat (2) wherever the design calls for it.

7. With the same silver-palegold mixture, stencil (3) always very brightly at the leaf tips, but shading quickly to black before you touch other units of the design.

8. With silver powder, stencil (4) and (5).

9. For the flange border, start with (6) at the handlehole, and alternate with (7) all around the tray, using palegold.

10. The last part of the powder work is to "cloud" *faintly* in silver the outer edges of both the floor and the flange borders. When clouding the floor, use a piece of tracing linen to protect the flange border. When this work is completed, lift the center piece of linen, and let the tray dry for 24 hours.

11. With pen and ink, draw the detail of the *center* flower on each of the four sides of the floor border. See Plate 20 for this detail.

Mix several showcard brushfuls of varnish with a little Alizarin Crimson and a touch of Burnt Umber, and apply the transparent red overtone to all the large flowers other than the four center ones. When this has reached the tacky stage, stencil (8) with palegold powder in the center of each of the eight red flowers. Allow 24 hours for drying.

12. Following the guide in Plate 20, do the hairline striping in mustard yellow.

13. Finish the tray in the usual way.

31 Stenciled Bread Tray

PLATE 21—PHOTO. IV (BETWEEN PP. 22-23)

1. Prepare the tray with three or four coats of flat black.

2. Trace the stencil units, depicted in Plate 21, on linen in the usual way. Note that (1) is a silhouette stencil. In this case, after the fruits are cut out, the linen is cut off around the outer edge.

3. Cut the stencils and number them as in the drawing. (This pattern should, of course, be done first on black paper for practice.)

4. Cut out a piece of linen which will exactly cover the floor of the tray, and extend up and cover the parts of the end pieces which are not to be decorated. The outline should first be carefully drawn on tracing paper, and then transferred to the linen. Fold where indicated in the sketch. Now varnish the tray for stenciling. When the varnish is tacky, the prepared piece of linen is laid in position on the tray floor, protecting it and the two curved edge segments at each end.

5. Place the cornucopia (1) in position, and stencil the fruit in silver. Then apply silver all around the edge of the linen to a depth of roughly ¼ to ½ inch. Next, pick up palegold powder, and going over the silver again, work on outward to the edge of the tray, and to the other edges of the area, so that a background of silver and gold is created for the cornucopia. Use a piece of linen to protect each side of the tray in turn from getting powdered. Stencil the other end of the bread tray in the same way.

Stencil (2) in silver in the center of each side. Then add the acorns (3), the leaves (4), and lastly the veins (5), all in silver. With palegold, cloud the ends and the outer edge of the side areas, going right out to the edge of the tray, but leaving some black all around the leaves.

To apply the curved gold lines on the black cornucopia, indicated on Plate 21 by the dotted line areas, use a "spit-brush." Take a small quill brush, wet it with saliva, and pick up loose gold powder the full length of the brush. Apply the powder on the still tacky surface.

Remove the linen from the tray floor. Let the work dry for 24 hours.

6. Give the tray a protective coat of varnish. Allow another 24 hours for drying.

7. Make a tracing of the freehand berries and leaf strokes in the drawing, and transfer them to the tray.

8. Mix Alizarin Crimson and Burnt Umber to make a transparent dark

86

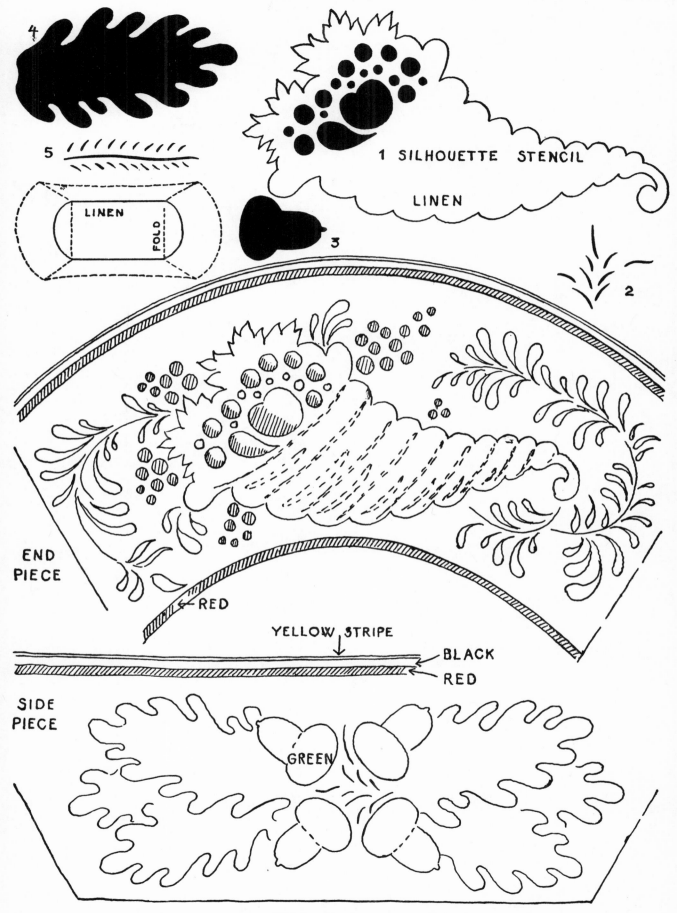

4

5

LINEN
FOLD

1 SILHOUETTE STENCIL

LINEN

3

2

END
PIECE

←RED

YELLOW STRIPE

BLACK
RED

SIDE
PIECE

GREEN

PLATE 21 STENCILED BREAD TRAY

red, and paint the shaded areas of the cornucopia fruit, blending off the edges of the color. Paint the berries outside the cornucopia.

Mix Indian Yellow and Prussian Blue to make a transparent green, and paint the leaves and stems, also the lower part of the acorns. Wait 24 hours.

9. Using transparent dark red, paint a stripe ⅛ inch wide along the lower edge of the end designs. Likewise paint a stripe ⅛ inch wide and ⅛ inch from the edge, all around the top edge of the tray. Allow 24 hours for drying.

10. With Japan Black and varnish, paint out the gold beyond the red stripe, so as to leave a black band ⅛ inch wide all around the edge of the tray. Wait 24 hours.

11. Paint a hairline mustard yellow stripe all around the floor of the tray, and around the top edge of the tray. Wait 24 hours.

12. Finish the tray in the usual way.

32 Stenciled Watering Can

PLATE 22A—PHOTO. VIII (BETWEEN PP. 22-23)

To make a copy of this pattern on black paper, proceed as follows:

1. Trace and cut the stencil units as shown in Plate 22A, making separate stencils for the veins. Number the units as in the illustration, and also mark on each the colored powder to be used with it.

2. Varnish a piece of black paper measuring about 12 by 14 inches, and when this has reached the proper tacky stage proceed to stencil, using the little layout on Plate 22A as a guide.

3. Place unit (1) in position, and stencil in palegold.

Stencil (2) in fire, very bright around the edges of the cut-outs, but leaving the centers black. Stencil (3), also in fire, but stopping short of (2) already stenciled. Do the veins in silver.

The leaves (4) are done in palegold, very bright around the edges, but shading quickly to black. Do not stencil into the flowers, but leave some black all around them. The leaf veins are in silver.

The flower (5) is stenciled in silver, and repeated several times as shown in the layout. Units (6), (7) and (8) are done next in that order, all in palegold.

In decorating a watering can, unit (5) is stenciled at the center of the handle, and the handle unit is added on each side of it.

If you decorate a box with this pattern, the handle unit might be used as a border around the sides of the box. Striping would be in mustard yellow.

90

2 FIRE 3

VEINS — SILVER

4
PALEGOLD

LAYOUT

HANDLE

5 SILVER

6
PALEGOLD

7

1 PALEGOLD

8
PALEGOLD

PLATE 22A   STENCILED WATERING CAN

33 *Stenciled Candle Holder*

PLATE 22B—PHOTO. VIII (BETWEEN PP. 22-23)

Photograph VIII shows a candle holder painted black with two stencil borders, the details of which are given in Plate 22B.

The flowers of the upper border are done in silver, and the rest in palegold. Apply both colors to each unit of this border before lifting the stencil and moving on to the next unit.

The lower border is in silver with a transparent green (Indian Yellow and Prussian Blue) overtone put on after the silver stenciling is completely dry.

PLATE 22B   BORDERS FOR STENCILED CANDLE HOLDER

93

34 Stenciled Spice Box

PLATE 23

The original spice box contained six small canisters, to which access was obtained by means of two sloping lids, one on each side of the handle. Each lid was decorated with the same scene.

1. Prepare the box with three or four coats of flat black.

2. Trace and cut the six stencil units shown in heavy black in Plate 23. Number them to correspond with the numbers in the Plate. (Naturally this pattern should be carried out first on black paper, by way of practice.)

3. Varnish the box for stenciling.

4. When the proper tacky stage has been reached, place unit (1) in position, and stencil in palegold. Next, stencil the little tree once on each side in palegold. Then do the fence behind the tree, also in palegold. The mountain (4) was done in silver, bright where the shading is shown in the upper drawing, but fading off quickly to black. There were faint touches of silver clouding in the sky, and of gold clouding on the ground.

The two long sides of the box were decorated with border stencil (5) in palegold.

On the ends, the group of figures (6) were done in palegold.

5. Fine striping was done in mustard yellow around each of the four sides.

PLATE 23 STENCILED SPICE BOX

35 *Stenciled Chair Patterns*

PLATES 24-25—PHOTOS. VI-VII (BETWEEN PP. 22-23)

PATTERN A

To make a copy of this pattern on black paper, proceed as follows:

1. Trace and cut the stencil units shown in Plate 24. Mark each unit with its number and the name of the colored powder to be used for it.

2. Varnish two sheets of black paper, one 13 by 3 inches, and the other 10 by 2½ inches.

3. When the varnished surface has reached the proper tacky stage, place stencil unit (1) in position, using the photograph as a guide. Stencil it in palegold, very bright on the upper half and around the lower edge. Lift stencil, and picking up a speck of fire powder on a clean part of the velvet, barely touch the center of the flower with a faint "cloud" of fire.

Stencil (2) and (3) in deepgold. Numbers (4) and (5) are in palegold with their centers faintly "clouded" with fire. Continue with the other units in numerical order.

For the smaller slat, start with (17) in palegold, then faintly cloud the center with fire; (18) is also in palegold, but fades off to black where it goes behind (17). Continue with (19) and (20). The leaf (6) is placed at each end, and the finishing touches are given by the tiny leaves (15) and (16).

1
PALEGOLD

2
DEEPGOLD
11

10
FIRE

SIDE
POST

3
DEEPGOLD
12

4   5
PALEGOLD

18 PALEGOLD

20 FIRE

8
DEEP
GOLD

9
DEEP
GOLD

6
DEEPGOLD
14

15
DEEPGOLD
16

17
PALEGOLD

7
DEEPGOLD
13

19
DEEPGOLD

PLATE 24   STENCILED CHAIR

PATTERN B

To make a copy of this pattern on black paper, proceed as follows:

1. Trace and cut the stencil units as shown in Plate 25. Then number the units as in the illustration, and mark them with the names of the colored powder or powders to be used for each.

2. Varnish two pieces of black paper, one 12½ by 4¼ inches, and the other 11 by 3 inches.

3. When the paper has reached the proper tacky stage, place stencil unit (1) in position, using the photograph as a guide. Stencil it in palegold, very bright on the upper half and around the lower edge. Lift stencil, pick up a speck of fire powder on a clean part of the velvet, and barely touch the center of the flower with a faint "cloud" of fire.

Stencil (2) in palegold, one on each side, and then faintly "cloud" the centers with fire. Stencil the melon (4) at the top center next, making it very bright palegold at the top, shading quickly to fire, and then to black behind the flower (1) already stenciled.

Then stencil the spray (3) in deep gold, once on each side. Next the melon (4) is repeated once on each side in palegold and fire. Continue with (5), (6), and (7), all in deepgold.

For the smaller slat, start with the border (8), doing it on each end in deepgold. Then place (9) in position at the center, stenciling it in palegold. Continue with the spray (10), placing it on each side. Next stencil the melon (11) on each side in bright palegold at the tips, shading quickly to fire, and thence to black. Last of all, add the leaf (12) on each side in deepgold.

OTHER BORDER PATTERNS

Additional patterns for furniture and tray borders are shown in Plates 26 and 27.

1 PALEGOLD

DEEPGOLD
5   7

SIDE POST

4
PALEGOLD & FIRE

6 DEEPGOLD
8

DEEPGOLD
3

2 PALEGOLD

10
PALEGOLD

13

DEEPGOLD
12

PALEGOLD
9

PALEGOLD & FIRE
11

SEAT FRONT

PLATE 25 STENCILED CHAIR

CUT SEPARATE STENCIL FOR VEIN

STENCILED TRAY BORDERS

PLATE 26   STENCILED FURNITURE AND (LOWER) TRAY BORDERS

SIDE POST 1

SEAT FRONT 2

CENTER

CHAIR SLAT

4

SEAT FRONT 3

5

BORDER UNIT

PLATE 27 FURNITURE STENCILS

36 Lace-Edge Tray

PLATE 28—PHOTO. XVI (BETWEEN PP. 38-39)

Lace-edge trays, round, oval, and rectangular in shape, date from about 1770. They were of English manufacture and were popular in America until well into the first half of the nineteenth century. Fruits and flowers were favorite subjects for decorating these trays, and great use was made of transparent tones of colors to give rich effects. The trays usually have a delicate gold leaf border around the edge of the floor. The more elaborate ones often had "tortoise shell" backgrounds and scattered clusters of small blue and white flowers, some of them almost disappearing into the background. The pattern given here is a more simple one, but nevertheless one of my own favorites.

To copy the center pattern, put a piece of frosted acetate over Plate 28, and proceed as follows:

1. With a mixture of off-white, paint the overall areas of the peach and strawberry, covering all detail and shading.

With a bluish country green (Japan Green, Prussian Blue, Raw Umber, and a touch of White), paint all the leaves which are shown in black. Wait 24 hours.

2. Squeeze out Indian Yellow, Alizarin Crimson, Burnt Umber, and Prussian Blue on a newspaper palette for use in floating color. Apply slow varnish to the peach with a showcard brush, wipe off the brush, and then, after picking up some dry yellow, brush it over the center of the peach, covering about two-thirds of the fruit. Add a speck of blue to the yellow to make a pale green and brush over the dotted section. Brush Alizarin Crimson with a touch of Burnt Umber over the shaded section, making it a deep red, which should be darker and browner where the cross-hatching is. The color thus blends from yellow to orange, to red, to deep reddish brown, and then to red again on the left-hand side of the peach.

Apply slow varnish to the strawberry. Brush yellow over the center, adding Alizarin Crimson and Burnt Umber over the shaded areas. Let the work dry for at least a week.

3. With off-white, paint all the leaves and stems and tiny brush strokes which are white in Plate 28. Add blue to the mixture to make a pale blue, and paint the shaded brush strokes.

With a thin mixture of off-white, paint the highlights on the green leaves. Wiping the brush back and forth on the newspaper until it is

102

GOLD LEAF BORDER

BLACK BACKGROUND

PLATE 28 LACE EDGE TRAY

rather "dry," go lightly over the face of the peach to give it a slightly downy look. Using a somewhat thicker mixture of off-white, but still keeping the brush "dry," go lightly around the edge of the peach, as shown by the whisker-like lines in the drawing, so as to soften the edge. Use a darker off-white on the shadow side. Do the same with the left edge of the berry. Paint the strawberry dots in off-white.

With a thin mixture of Burnt Umber, paint a stroke on the dark side of each large green and white leaf.

37 Chippendale Tray

PLATES 29 AND 30—PHOTO. XVII (BETWEEN PP. 38-39)

Chippendale trays, also known as Gothic trays and Pie Crust trays, originated about 1760, during the Chippendale furniture period. They continued to be manufactured for more than a century and were immensely popular during the Victorian era, when there was a Chippendale revival.

These trays were never stenciled. Some of the earlier ones were decorated with elaborate gold borders, while the center was left blank. Trays of the later period, however, were quite showy, and much use was made of brilliant transparent overtones of rich color in the painting of flowers and of gorgeous birds.

The small tray shown in Photo. XVII measures 9¾ by 12¾ inches and has a gold leaf scroll border, while the birds and fountain basin have a gold leaf base. Make a practice copy of the floor design (Plate 29), using pale-gold powder for this purpose instead of gold leaf.

1. With Japan Vermilion, paint the birds and the basin, disregarding all details. When tacky, apply the gold powder. Dry 24 hours.

2. Mix some Japan Vermilion, Burnt Umber, and White to make a medium deep pink, and with this mixture, paint the large rose A, disregarding all detail. Wipe off the brush and apply a little extra Burnt Umber to darken the areas indicated by broken lines in the illustration. Using the same deep pink, paint the smaller flowers marked B.

Paint the large flower C in Japan Vermilion, blending in a little dry Burnt Umber to darken the center.

With a mixture of Country Green, paint all the leaves, stems, and brush strokes representing small leaves. Wait 24 hours.

3. Mix Prussian Blue and Raw Umber to make a transparent blue, and paint the wings on the bird D; also the head and breast, blending off the lower edge of the blue with a clear varnish brush.

Mix some Alizarin Crimson and Burnt Umber to make a rich transparent red, and paint the wings of the bird E, blending off the color. Mix a little Prussian Blue and Indian Yellow to make light green, and apply this to the back of the bird, blending off the color towards the tail.

Apply slow varnish to the rose A. Wipe off the brush, and then lightly brush some dry Alizarin Crimson and Burnt Umber into the flower to

106

PLATE 29 CHIPPENDALE TRAY—A

produce a deeper pink, darkening the shaded areas with a still darker pink, almost brown.

Apply slow varnish to the red flower C, and immediately brush in a little Alizarin Crimson and Burnt Umber over the entire flower, adding a bit more pigment in the center and around the upper edge to darken those parts. This completes the floating color in this pattern.

Mix a little Alizarin Crimson and Burnt Umber to make a deep pink, and apply this to all the smaller flowers B. Allow the work to dry. The slow varnish takes at least a week to dry, but after 48 hours it is dry enough for you to continue on other parts of the pattern.

4. Add enough varnish to off-white to make a transparent white, and apply this to the tail of the bird D. Wipe the brush, and then picking up some fairly dry White, paint several long, thin strokes on the wet surface to suggest tail feathers. Do the same on the other bird.

Using the same thin off-white, paint the water in the fountain, adding some dry White here and there to accent it.

Apply a transparent overtone of Burnt Umber to one side of each leaf, blending off the inner edge. With a semi-transparent mustard yellow, paint the highlights on the leaves and the brush-strokes in the crest of bird D. Wait 24 hours.

5. Paint the veins of the leaves with Japan Black.

6. When the two large flowers are completely dry, mix a thick off-white to accent the edges of the rose petals. Paint one petal at a time, immediately using a second brush with a little varnish on it to blend and soften the inner edge of the white. Do the same with the smaller flowers and buds.

With a somewhat thinner mixture of off-white, paint the white curved lines on the bird D, the eyes of both birds, and the petal lines on the flower C. Let dry 24 hours.

To decorate a tray:

1. Paint the tray flat black in the usual way.

2. Apply a thin film of whiting in preparation for gold leaf.

3. Make a tracing of the pattern from Plates 29 and 30, and transfer the gold sections to the tray.

4. With the Yellow Ochre and varnish, paint the gold sections of the floor design, the scroll border, and the stripe around the edge. When tacky, lay the gold leaf. Wait one week.

5. Apply a protective coat of varnish. Wait 24 hours.

6. Transfer the rest of the pattern to the tray, following the directions given above for the practice copy.

7. Finish the tray in the usual way.

PLATE 30   CHIPPENDALE TRAY—B

38 Large Oval Tray

Oval trays of the kind shown in the colored frontispiece were first made in England during the Victorian period. This one had a scroll border done in palegold bronze powder, with touches of dark blue. The flowers are mostly in floating color. Good practice may be obtained by first making a copy of the pattern on frosted acetate.

1. On tracing paper, make a complete tracing of the pattern from Plates 31, 32, and 33. Mount this on white cardboard, so that the lines can be seen easily, and put a sheet of frosted acetate over it.

2. Mix White, Raw Umber, and Yellow Ochre to make a pale beige, and paint the overall area of the rose A, disregarding all detail. In the same way, do the small rose G, and the bud F.

Adding more Yellow Ochre to the mixture to make a deep cream, paint the rose B.

With a mixture of off-white, paint the morning-glory C, its buds D, and the blossoms and buds E, H, and K.

With Vermilion, paint the flowers M and N. Wait 24 hours.

3. With a dark bluish country green (Japan Green, Prussian Blue, and Raw Umber), paint all the black areas in the illustrations, disregarding details.

With a yellowish country green (Japan Green, Japan Yellow, and Burnt Umber), paint all the other leaves, buds, and stems. Wait 24 hours.

4. On a newspaper palette, squeeze out Alizarin Crimson, Burnt Umber, Indian Yellow, Prussian Blue, and Raw Umber in preparation for floating color. This procedure involves the application of slow varnish to a flower with a showcard brush. (Refer to Chapter 9 for full general directions on floating color.) Wiping off the brush with a cloth, pick up a tiny speck of the requisite undiluted color, and lightly brush it on the flower, as follows:

Rose A. Brush in Indian Yellow over the middle and lower parts. Then brush Alizarin Crimson and Burnt Umber over those parts that are shaded in the illustration to make them a rose color, using more pigment to darken the part under the "cup" of the rose, and in the "heart" of the rose. Do the same with G and F.

Rose B. Brush in the yellow all over the flower. Then add a touch of

110

PLATE 31 LARGE OVAL TRAY—A

the blue in the shaded parts to make a pale green, adding a little Burnt Umber for the darker parts of the rose.

Blossoms E. Brush green (Indian Yellow and Prussian Blue) in the centers. Add rose color over the shaded areas, accenting the petals with Burnt Umber.

Morning-glory C. Brush the yellow in the center, adding a hint of green here and there, but keeping it all very light. Then brush blue (Prussian Blue and Raw Umber) over the rest of the flower, applying the brush strokes from the center out to the edges, and making the color a bit darker here and there.

Buds D. Brush blue over the tips, and Raw Umber at the upper ends, applying little and lightly for pale effects in both cases.

Flower H. Brush blue over the shaded areas for a medium blue effect, adding a darker touch to the center.

Flowers K. Brush blue lightly for a pale effect over the shaded areas, adding a little Raw Umber on one side of each flower.

Wait at least a week for the floating color to dry properly.

5. Give the shaded areas on all the leaves, the green rosebud, and the calyx on F, an overtone of Burnt Sienna, blending off the edges with varnish.

Give the shaded areas on the flowers M and N an overtone of transparent dark red (Alizarin Crimson and Burnt Umber), blending the edges here and there. Allow 24 hours to dry.

6. When the slow-varnish parts are completely dry, apply the off-white veiling on the roses A, B, F, and G (see p. 34). White veiling should also be used to highlight some of the petals on the blossoms E.

Mix Japan Yellow and White for a pale yellow, and paint the dots on the flowers E, H, and M, and the little drops on the flowers K; also the dots under the green rosebud and the tear drops on the extreme right.

With Burnt Umber, paint the veins in the leaves as shown in the drawings (not the dotted line veins). Wait 24 hours.

7. With dark red (Alizarin Crimson and Burnt Umber), paint the brush strokes in the heart of the rose A and those on the rose B; also the strokes marked R on the morning-glory. Paint touches of dark red on some of the yellow dots in the flowers E and K.

Mix a thin Yellow Ochre with White, and paint the dotted line strokes on the leaves and green buds, and also those on the flowers N.

To decorate a tray with this pattern:

1. Paint the tray flat black in the usual way.

2. Turn the tray upside down on a large sheet of tracing paper, and trace a line around the edge to get the oval shape. Mark the centers of top and bottom, and of both ends, and trace there the center border motif X, shown in Plate 34. Likewise mark the centers of the four quarters,

PLATE 32   LARGE OVAL TRAY—B

and trace there the motif Y. Using the colored photograph (see frontis-piece) as a guide, fill in the scroll sections along the edge, making any needed adjustments, and tracing on the wrong side of the paper when required.

3. Transfer the border to the tray (see Chapter 11).

4. With Japan Vermilion paint the scrolls, all of which are white on Plate 34. As you paint along, stop from time to time to apply palegold powder to those parts which have become tacky. Allow 24 hours to dry. The original tray had no gold stripe around the edge.

5. Mix Prussian Blue, Raw Umber, and White to get a deep blue and paint the areas shown in black on Plate 34. Apply touches of transparent Burnt Sienna here and there on the scrolls. Leave to dry for 24 hours.

6. Give the tray a coat of varnish to protect the border.

7. Transfer the center design to the tray, and paint it as described above for the acetate copy.

8. Finish the tray in the usual way.

PLATE 33   LARGE OVAL TRAY—C

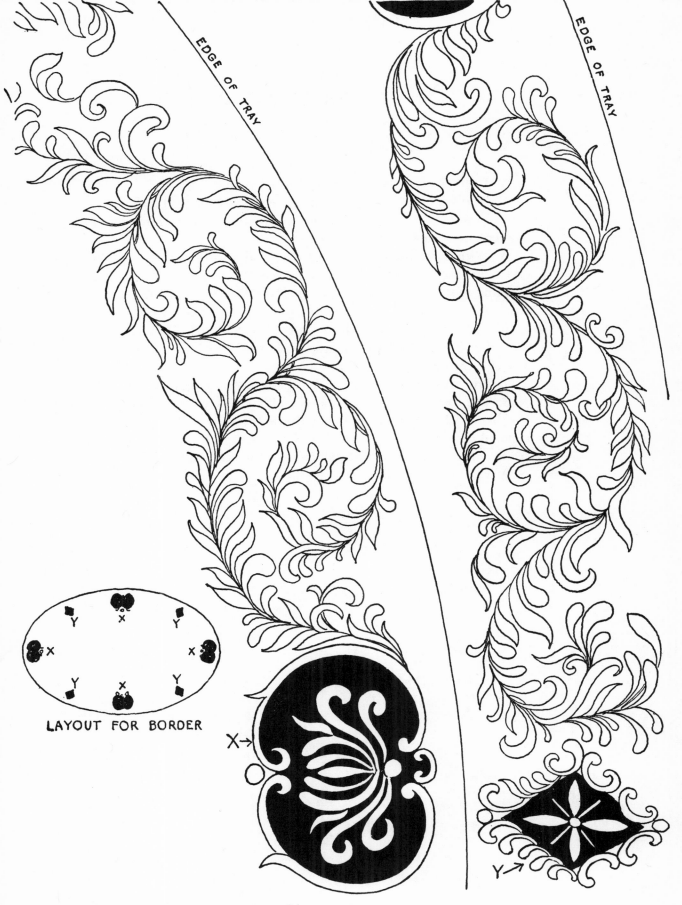

EDGE OF TRAY

EDGE OF TRAY

LAYOUT FOR BORDER

X→

Y→

PLATE 34   LARGE OVAL TRAY—D

39 "Queen Anne" Tray

PLATES 6 AND 35—PHOTO. XVIII (BETWEEN PP. 38-39)

1. Paint the tray flat black in the usual way.

2. Apply a thin film of whiting in preparation for gold leaf.

3. From Plates 6 and 35, trace the pattern, and transfer to the tray the sections which are to be done in gold leaf.

4. With a mixture of Yellow Ochre and varnish, paint those sections which are to be gold, doing first the center part, and then the border, omitting the dots which are *black* in Plate 35. Paint the stripe around the edge. When all this is tacky, lay the gold leaf. Wait one week.

5. Apply a coat of varnish to protect the gold leaf. Wait 24 hours.

6. Go over the surface lightly with steel wool to remove the gloss. Transfer the rest of the design to the tray.

7. Proceed to paint the flowers as described in pages 32-34.

8. The shaded areas of the border (Plate 35) are in transparent Burnt Umber, which should be applied with one brush stroke each time, and then blended off on one side with a clear varnish brush. The dots which are shown in black should be painted in off-white. Wait 24 hours.

9. Finish the tray in the usual way.

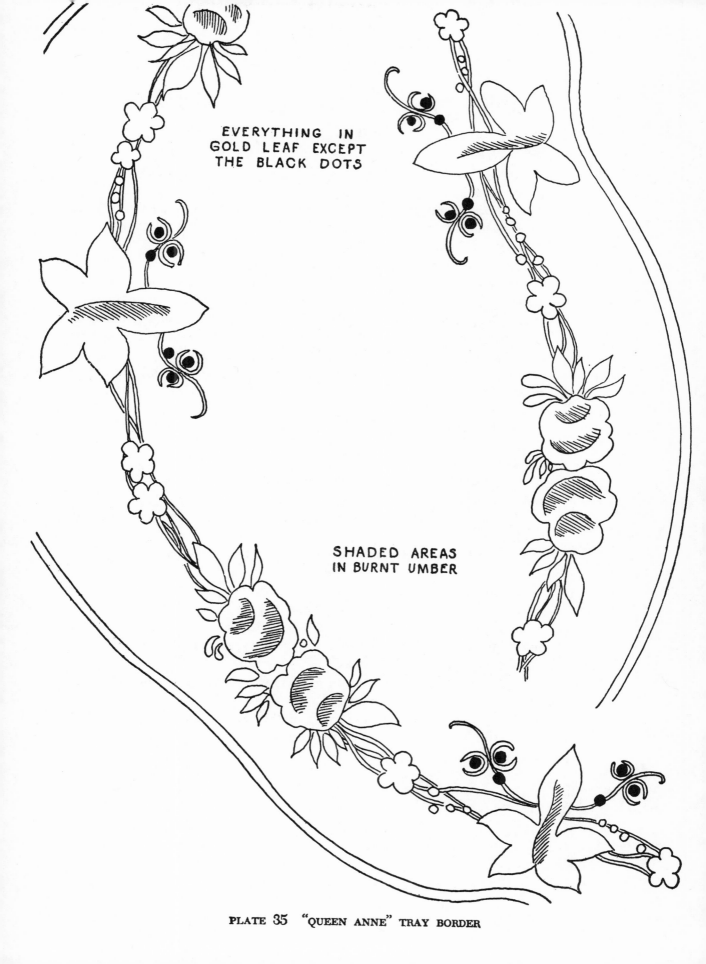

EVERYTHING IN
GOLD LEAF EXCEPT
THE BLACK DOTS

SHADED AREAS
IN BURNT UMBER

PLATE 35 "QUEEN ANNE" TRAY BORDER

40   Rectangular Gold Leaf Tray

PLATES 36 AND 37—PHOTO. XIV (BETWEEN PP. 38-39)

Rectangular trays date from about 1760 and were made in all sizes. They were popular for at least a century, and all styles of decoration were used on them.

1. Paint the tray flat black in the usual way.

2. Apply a thin film of whiting in preparation for gold leaf.

3. Trace the flower sprays on Plate 36, using separate pieces of tracing paper for each to facilitate handling. Transfer the tracings to the tray, using the photograph as a guide. Next, make a tracing of the section of borders in the upper part of Plate 37, and transfer that also to the tray, repeating until the border is completely around the tray.

4. With a mixture of Yellow Ochre and varnish, paint all the design which is to be gold, doing one section at a time. Everything is gold except the flower centers and the inner parts of their petals. Disregard all the black brush-strokes and leaf veins shown in the drawings.

If the entire tray is too much to do at one time, leave some parts for another day. The fine gold line work on the flange is quite easily done with a striping quill. Note there is no gold stripe to be painted around the edge of the tray.

5. When the proper tacky stage has been reached, lay the gold leaf. Wait one week.

6. Apply a coat of varnish to the tray to protect the gold. Wait 24 hours.

7. Rub gently with steel wool to remove the gloss. With a mixture of off-white, paint the flower centers and the insides of the flower petals. With Japan Black, paint the black brush strokes over the gold along the inner edge of the border. Also paint the leaf veins and shadings, which are shown in black in Plate 36. Wait 24 hours.

8. With a mixture of varnish, Alizarin Crimson, and a touch of Burnt Umber, paint the transparent red overtones on the off-white petals and flower centers where indicated by the broken lines in the same Plate.

9. Add a mustard yellow stripe around the edge of the tray, and finish in the usual way.

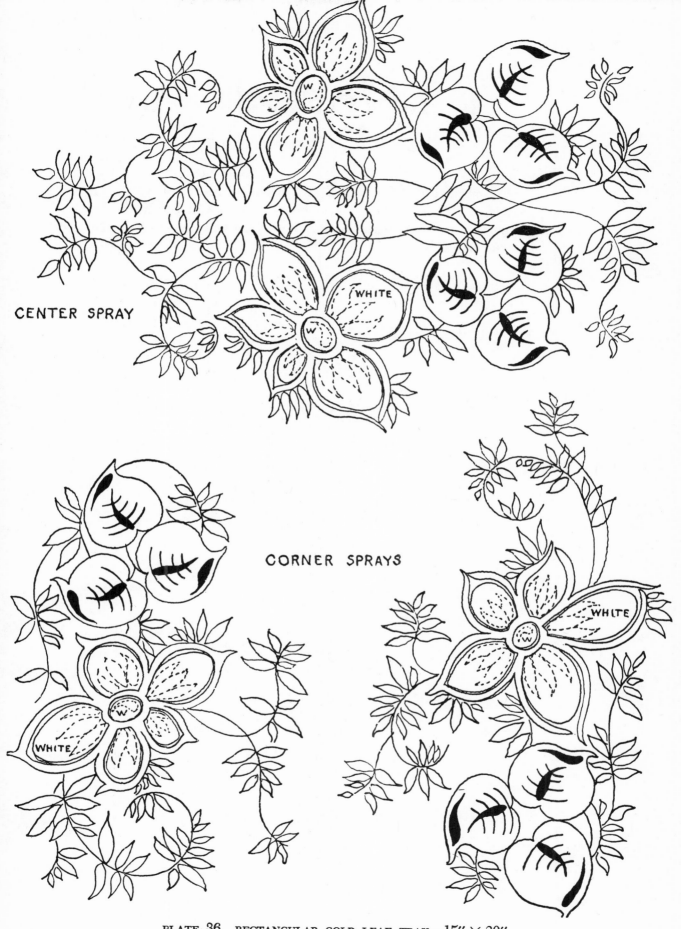

CENTER SPRAY

CORNER SPRAYS

WHITE

W

WHITE

W

WHITE

W

PLATE 36   RECTANGULAR GOLD LEAF TRAY—15" × 20"

41 Large Oval Gold Leaf Tray

PLATE 37

The original of this tray was very large and had a rolled edge. It was painted black, and the border design was done in gold leaf. In the drawing the gold parts are shown in black. The edging was painted over the gold in a creamy white.

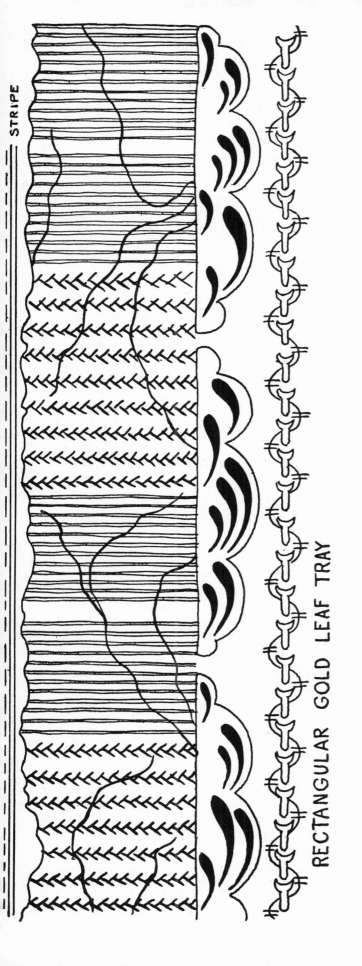

STRIPE

RECTANGULAR GOLD LEAF TRAY

WHITE

GOLD LEAF

EDGE OF TRAY

PLATE 37   GOLD LEAF TRAYS—(UPPER) RECTANGULAR; (LOWER) LARGE OVAL.

42   Gold Leaf Box

PLATE 38—PHOTO. XII (BETWEEN PP. 38-39)

1. Paint the box flat black in the usual way.

2. Trace the design from Plate 38, making any adjustments that may be necessary to suit the size and shape of the box. Transfer the tracing to the box.

3. With a mixture of Yellow Ochre and varnish, paint the design, with the exception of the small round berries shown black in the drawing. Cover all the details and the shaded areas. Paint also the border stripes on the top and sides of the box. When the proper tacky stage has been reached, lay the gold leaf. Wait one week.

4. Apply a coat of varnish to the box to protect the gold leaf. Let it dry 24 hours.

5. Rub lightly with steel wool to remove gloss. With a crow-quill pen and black ink, draw the leaf veins, the shading on the leaves and stems, and the cross-hatching and detail on the acorns. Wait half an hour for the ink to harden.

6. Mix some varnish with a little Indian Yellow and Prussian Blue to make a transparent green. Taking the parts marked G on the group of leaves at the top of the pattern as a guide, paint a green area on each leaf there and elsewhere. Apply the green with one or two strokes, blending off the edges. Also apply a touch of green over the cross-hatching on the acorns.

Paint the small round berries in Vermilion. Wait 24 hours.

7. Mix Burnt Umber and varnish to get a transparent brown, and taking the parts marked U on the group of leaves at the top of the pattern as the example, paint similar patches here and there at discretion on all the other leaves. On some leaves add brown to the center vein. There is also a touch of brown along one side of each acorn.

8. Finish the box in the usual way.

G - TRANSPARENT GREEN
U -   "   BURNT UMBER

PLATE 38   GOLD LEAF BOX

43 Small Oval Gold Leaf Tray

PLATE 39—PHOTO. XIX (BETWEEN PP. 38-39)

1. Paint the tray flat black in the usual way.

2. Turn the tray face down on tracing paper, and draw a line around the edge of the tray to get its shape. Put this tracing over the sprays on Plate 39 to see whether they fit your oval. Trace the sprays around the edge of the oval, making any necessary adjustments. Refer to the photograph.

3. With a mixture of Yellow Ochre and varnish, paint the design, including the stripe. When the work is tacky, lay the gold leaf. Wait one week.

4. Apply a coat of varnish to protect the gold leaf. Allow 24 hours for drying.

5. Rub gently with steel wool to remove the gloss. Paint the dots and veins in black. Wait 24 hours.

6. With a transparent brown, made of Burnt Umber and varnish, paint the shaded areas. Wait 24 hours.

7. Finish the tray in the usual way.

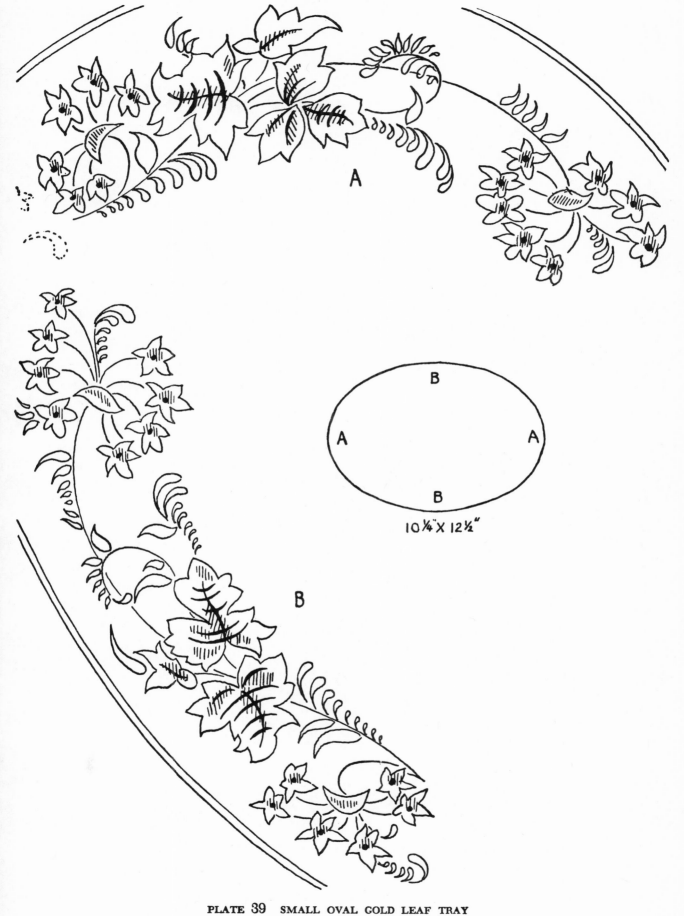

A

B

B

A A

B

10¼"X 12½"

B

PLATE 39   SMALL OVAL GOLD LEAF TRAY

TOP OF STILES

CHEST OF
DRAWERS

SEAT FRONT

HITCHCOCK   HAND GRIP

PLATE 40   GOLD LEAF FURNITURE MOTIFS

Index

(Italic numbers refer to pages on which illustrations appear)

131